Lectures on Language
Contact

Lectures on Language
Contact   Ilse Lehiste

The MIT Press
Cambridge, Massachusetts
London, England

© 1988 Massachusetts Institute of Technology

All rights reserved. No part of this book may be reproduced in any form by any electronic or mechanical means (including photocopying, recording, or information storage and retrieval) without permission in writing from the publisher.

This book was set in Times Roman by Graphic Composition, Inc. and printed and bound by Halliday Lithograph in the United States of America.

Library of Congress Cataloging-in-Publication Data

Lehiste, Ilse
  Lectures on language contact.
  Bibliography; p.
  Includes index.
  1. Languages in contact. 2. Interference (Linguistics)
3. Languages, Mixed. I. Title.
P130.5.L44 1988   401'.9   87-29404
ISBN 0-262-12131-X
ISBN 0-262-62061-8 (pbk.)

Contents

Preface   vii

Chapter 1
The Concept of Interference   1

Chapter 2
Bilingualism: The Bilingual Individual   28

Chapter 3
Bilingualism: The Bilingual Community   44

Chapter 4
Language Contact and Linguistic Convergence   59

Chapter 5
Results of Language Contact: Pidgins and Creoles   76

Glossary   93

Bibliography   97

Index   117

Preface

The following materials represent condensed lecture notes for a course that I developed and taught at The Ohio State University from 1973 to 1984. The course covered most aspects of language contact, including ways in which languages enter into contact; the concept of linguistic affinity (Sprachbund); language contact as a cause for linguistic change; results of language contact: pidgins and creoles; methods of comparing linguistic structures; the concept of linguistic interference; the bilingual individual and the bilingual community. Obviously it is not possible to treat each topic in detail in a one-quarter course; but suggestions for additional reading are given after each chapter. The glossary provides definitions of basic concepts, and the bibliography contains additional references. The bibliography is not intended to be exhaustive; I have simply assembled a set of titles, most of which I have used in the preparation of my lectures on language contact. For this presentation in book form, I have updated the bibliography and integrated several new references into the text. I present these lecture notes with the hope that they may be useful for a colleague preparing to teach a course on language contact, perhaps for the first time.

My debt to two linguists who have dealt with language contact in a pioneering fashion is so great that it would constitute a sin of omission if I did not single them out at the beginning of these lecture notes. They are Uriel Weinreich and Einar Haugen. Sapienti sat.

Chapter 1
The Concept of Interference

Language contact takes place between speakers of different languages in contact situations. In order for communication to take place, speakers must arrive at a certain degree of comprehension of the other language and must acquire a degree of facility in producing utterances that will be comprehensible. In time, some speakers will be able to alternate between languages; they have become bilingual.

Frequently a person is considered bilingual if he can speak both of his languages in such a way that he cannot be distinguished from monolingual speakers of either language. This would be the ideal case, and it will be explained later why such cases are extremely rare. It is more realistic to allow for a wider range of facility with the two (or more) languages involved in the contact situation. The theoretical limits to bilingualism might be drawn to encompass the range between the person who uses one nonintegrated loanword and the so-called perfect bilingual who can pass for a monolingual in more than one language. For the moment I would like to define a *bilingual* as a person who is able to produce grammatical sentences in more than one language.

There are, nevertheless, degrees of correctness (if correctness is defined as perfect compliance with the norms of a language) in the production of these sentences by a bilingual. *Interference* frequently takes place, defined here as deviations from the norms of either language that occur in the speech of bilinguals as a result of their familiarity with more than one language.

Interference can be found at all levels: phonetics, phonology, morphology, syntax, semantics, and lexis. There are, of course, also degrees of interference. A perfect bilingual may switch from language to language during a conversation. This phenomenon is called *code switching;* again, in the ideal case all aspects are switched simultaneously. More frequently a certain degree of interference accompanies code switching. A sequence of steps often takes place: (1) A bilingual introduces a loanword from language A into language B in a phonetic form close to the norm of language A. (2) If the bilingual has occasion to repeat it, or if other speakers also begin using it, elements of language B will be substituted for those of language A. (3) If monolinguals learn the loanword, a total or practically total substitution will be made in the sound structure, and the word will be integrated into the grammar as well.

Phonic Interference

Phonic interference occurs when a bilingual perceives and reproduces the sounds of one language (the secondary language, language B) in terms of his primary language (language A). Interference arises when the bilingual identifies a phoneme of the secondary language with a phoneme of the primary language and, in reproducing it, subjects it to the phonetic rules of the primary language.

The most obvious kind of phonetic interference is *sound substitution*. This arises when phonemes that are identically defined in two languages have different phonetic realizations, and when the pronunciation of language A is carried over into language B. It is this kind of interference that is commonly referred to as *foreign accent*. For example, the phoneme /t/ is found in Slavic languages as well as in English, but in Slavic languages /t/ is normally dental (articulated with the tip of the tongue against the inner surface of the upper front teeth), whereas in English /t/ is normally alveolar (articulated with the

Concept of Interference

tip of the tongue against the alveolar ridge). In Slavic languages the phoneme /r/ is realized as a tongue-tip trill, whereas in American English /r/ is a retroflex continuant.

There are situations in which language A lacks a phoneme of language B, or in which language A has one phoneme, whereas language B has two phonemes, both of which bear some phonetic similarity to the phoneme present in language A. Interesting observations can be made regarding the sound substitutions chosen by speakers of the borrowing language. We assume that the speakers will try to substitute the sound that seems to them to be the "closest" sound to the one they are trying to match. Sometimes the substitutions are not at all obvious to speakers of other languages. For example, English has the phonemes /θ/ and /ð/, which are not found in French and Russian. Both French and Russian have the phonemes /s/, /z/, /t/, and /d/. Speakers of French choose /s/ and /z/ as substitutes for English /θ/ and /ð/, whereas speakers of Russian choose /t/ and /d/. To use conventional spelling, English *think* and *them* would be pronounced somewhat like *sink* and *zem* by a monolingual speaker of French and somewhat like *tink* and *dem* by a monolingual speaker of Russian. Both French and Russian use dental /t/-sounds; English /θ/ is an interdental fricative. Speakers of French have kept the fricative feature, whereas speakers of Russian have evidently considered that feature relatively unimportant. The answer to the puzzle may come from a comparison of the sound systems of all three languages.

Another example of substitution that may seem counterintuitive to a speaker of English may be found in the realization of English /t/ in Hindi. As noted, English /t/ is alveolar. Hindi lacks an alveolar consonant series, but it has a dental series and a retroflex series of stops. Speakers of Russian use their dental /t/ to realize English alveolar /t/; speakers of Hindi, however, choose their retroflex stop rather than the dental one to render the alveolar /t/ of English loanwords. They perceive English /t/ as resembling their own retroflex stop more than their dental stop.

Similar to sound substitution in its effects is the *transfer of rules* from one language to another. For example, German has a rule of final devoicing, according to which word-final (and in most cases morpheme-final) voiced obstruents are phonetically realized as their voiceless counterparts. English lacks such a rule. Speakers of German frequently carry this rule over when they pronounce English words such as *have* with a final [f], and they may be misunderstood as having said *half*. Failure to apply a rule that is required in a language by speakers of a language that does not have this rule is another source of foreign accent. For example, English has a rule requiring a syllable nucleus to be lengthened before a voiced final consonant within the same syllable; German does not have such a rule. Speakers of English can form a verb from the noun *house*—namely, *to house*—by voicing the final /s/ and lengthening the diphthong (substituting /z/ for /s/ and thus triggering the application of the lengthening rule). I have heard a speaker of German produce the verb *to house* with a voiceless final consonant and with no lengthening. (It remains uncertain whether the speaker intended to produce the English version of *to house* and failed to apply the rules, or whether he simply assumed that *house* can be turned into a verb without any phonetic modification.)

Another example of rule transfer resulting in perceived foreign accent might be the case of Slavic regressive voicing assimilation in obstruent clusters carried over into English. This rule applies to consonant clusters consisting of fricatives and plosives; the whole cluster acquires the voicing feature from its last member. A speaker of a Slavic language is likely to pronounce English phrases and compounds like *back down* and *ragtag* as *bag down* and *racktack*, respectively (many Slavic languages, including Russian, have a final devoicing rule similar to that of German). This particular rule is very persistent and may sometimes be observed even in the speech of second generation speakers of American English who have Slavic family background.

Other types of phonic interference involve mostly phonemic interpretations. The most important of these is *underdifferentiation*. Underdifferentiation is likely to take place when language A lacks a contrast that is present in language B: two sounds are confused in the secondary system, if their phonetic counterparts are not distinguished in the primary system. Expressed in other terms, underdifferentiation will occur when two sounds that are allophones of a phoneme in language A are separate phonemes in language B. Underdifferentiation may also be due to different phonotactic rules in the two languages.

An example of the latter kind of interference may be found in comparing English and Spanish. English has no restrictions on the occurrence of nasals in final position: -*m#*, -*n#*, and -*ŋ#* are all possible. Spanish has only -*n#*, and speakers of Spanish have considerable difficulty in identifying and pronouncing final nasals when they are learning English. Other examples of underdifferentiation may be found in comparing Germanic and Finno-Ugric languages. English distinguishes between [s] and [ʃ]; Finnish has only one voiceless sibilant, which is phonetically roughly intermediate between the two sounds occurring in English. Speakers of Finnish continually make mistakes in English sibilants. Germanic languages also possess a voicing correlation in consonants (for example, English and German distinguish between /g/ and /k/ in initial position); Balto-Finnic languages lack the correlation. A speaker of Estonian will have great difficulty in learning the systematic distinctions between voiced and voiceless consonants (for example, German *Garten* 'garden' versus *Karten* 'cards').

Underdifferentiation contributes strongly to a perceived foreign accent. *Overdifferentiation,* on the other hand, is not normally perceived by listeners, even though the speaker may be overdifferentiating in production. Overdifferentiation is the imposition of phonemic distinctions from the primary system on the sounds of the secondary system. In other words, allophones of the secondary system are treated as phonemes because they are phonemes in the primary system.

For example, both Spanish and English possess the sounds [d] and [ð]. In English they are distinct phonemes; in Spanish they are allophones of a single phoneme, [ð] occurring in intervocalic position,

[d] in initial position and in intervocalic clusters following [n]. Speakers of English identify the two Spanish sounds with their phonemes /d/ and /ð/; they simply must learn the rules for the occurrence of the two phonemes. Speakers of Spanish, on the other hand, are likely to underdifferentiate: identifying the English sounds with the allophones of their single phoneme, they will apply the distribution rules that are found in their primary language.

Another kind of phonic interference is *reinterpretation of distinctions*. This type of interference takes place when the bilingual distinguishes phonemes of the secondary system by features that are distinctive in his primary system but are merely concomitant or redundant in the secondary system. For example, German has long and short vowels; there is a vowel quality difference in some of the short-long pairs, but it is the length that distinguishes between the two sets of vowels. English has no systematic length distinctions in its vowel system, although some vowels may be intrinsicially long and others intrinsically short. There is a vowel quality difference between intrinsically long and intrinsically short vowels produced at similar articulatory positions. Phonetically, the vowels in the German words *bieten* 'to offer' and *bitten* 'to request' are quite similar to the vowels in the English words *beat* and *bit;* in the German system this phonetic difference is redundant, whereas in the English system the length difference is redundant. Speakers of English may identify the German vowels by their phonetic quality rather than by their distinctive length.

On the other hand, English has a voicing distinction in final consonants, and vowel length depends on the presence or absence of voicing: *bead* has a longer vowel than *beat*. German has a final devoicing rule that neutralizes the distinction in final position; speakers of German may interpret the vowel length, which is a dependent variable in English, as phonemic.

Phonotactic interference was already mentioned as one cause of underdifferentiation. Phonotactic interference occurs when distributional restrictions of language A are carried over into language B. As an example, let us look at the treatment of loanwords from Slavic and Germanic into Finnish and Estonian. Indo-European languages have many words with initial consonant clusters; Finnic languages tolerate only a single initial consonant. Thus, an early loan from a Germanic word that survives in English as *strand* appears in Finnish and Estonian with a simplified initial cluster: *ranta* and *rand,* respectively. The early Slavic word *gramota* 'book' (from Greek *grammata* (pl.)) appears in Finnish as *raamattu* and in Estonian as *raamat*. (Incidentally, the treatment of initial clusters may serve to establish the relative age of loanwords, since later loanwords appear in Estonian with their initial clusters intact: German *Glas* 'glass' gives Estonian *klaas,* whereas in the more conservative Finnish, which continues to apply the old phonotactic rule, the loanword has the form *lasi.*)

Interference may also be observed in the treatment of suprasegmental features like tone, stress, and quantity, the last of which was already discussed in connection with the English and German vowel systems. The observations made above concerning types of interference also apply to suprasegmental systems. A speaker of a language wihout lexical tone is likely to underdifferentiate in producing words from a tone language and in learning to understand a tone language. Reinterpretation of distinctions frequently takes place: a syllable with high pitch can be heard as stressed by a speaker of a language in which heightened fundamental frequency is a phonetic characteristic of stressed syllables. Falling fundamental frequency is a phonetic feature of overlong syllables in Estonian; I have heard speakers of tone languages identify such overlong syllables with the distinctive falling tone of their own language.

Phonotactic interference can also be observed. Hungarian, for example, has initial stress, whereas German words are normally stressed on the first syllable of the stem; Hungarian accent is imitated in Vienna by shifting the stress to the initial syllable of every German word. Czech has initial stress, whereas Russian has movable stress; since the two languges are closely related, many Russian words have easily recognizable Czech counterparts. Speakers of Czech are likely to produce almost random stresses in speaking Russian, with one interesting modification: they tend to avoid initial stress, recognizing that initial stress is a Czech characteristic. This leads to *hypercorrection*, a phenomenon that plays a considerable part in situations involving language contact.

Phonic interference can be studied experimentally. As examples of the kinds of research that can be performed to investigate this aspect of language contact, let us consider a sequence of studies dealing with the production and perception of initial plosive consonants by monolinguals and bilinguals.

Cross-language studies have shown that voice onset time is a sufficient cue to separate initial stop consonants into phonemic categories. The experimental technique involves asking listeners to identify whether each of a series of stimuli contains a voiced or a voiceless plosive. In a large number of studies these stimuli have been synthetic monosyllables beginning with an initial plosive. The voice onset time has been systematically varied, so that the onset of periodicity (corresponding to the onset of vocal fold vibration) either precedes the release of the plosive consonant or follows it in calibrated steps. In one set of experiments (labeling tests) the listeners must identify the initial consonants of stimuli presented one at a time; in another set of experiments (discrimination tests) they must judge whether the members of a pair of stimuli are the same or different. We are currently concerned with the labeling task. Experiments have shown that listeners who are native speakers of English label stimuli as containing a voiced initial plosive when the onset of voice takes place at time intervals shorter than 25 msec after the release and as containing a voiceless initial plosive when the onset of voice takes place later than that. On the other hand, listeners whose native language is French or Spanish partition the continuum at a much shorter voice onset time; they label plosives with more than approximately 5 msec voicing delay as "voiceless."

A series of studies has been carried out with monolingual speakers of French, English, and Spanish, and with English-French and

English-Spanish bilinguals, to explore whether there is interference from one or the other language in the production and perception of voiced and voiceless initial plosives by bilinguals, and to establish whether there exist systematic differences between monolinguals and bilinguals in this regard.

Caramazza et al. (1973) studied both production and perception, using three groups of subjects: 10 monolingual Canadian French speakers, 10 monolingual Canadian English speakers, and 20 bilingual French-English speakers for whom French was the first or dominant language. Each testing session began by having the subject read aloud a set of English or French stop-initial words containing either of two members of a voiced-voiceless pair (for instance, *papillon–ballade*). The readings were recorded on tape and later analyzed acoustically; voice onset time was measured from spectrograms. After having produced the words, each subject was presented with a randomized sequence of synthesized monosyllables beginning with a plosive consonant and was asked to label the syllables as /ba/ or /pa/, /da/ or /ta/, or /ga/ or /ka/. The monolingual subjects read three sets of words and labeled each of the three stop continua. The bilingual subjects were tested twice, once in an English setting, with instructions in English, and once in a French setting. They thus produced six sets of words, three sets in English and three sets in French; they also labeled each of the three stop continua twice.

The results for the two monolingual groups confirmed existing knowledge: the English speakers produced aspirated voiceless plosives (with a relatively long voice onset time), and the French speakers produced unaspirated voiceless plosives, their voice onset taking place immediately after the release of the initial consonant. In perception, too, the two groups differed in a predictable manner: there was a statistically significant difference in the crossover points of the labeling functions for the two groups, and the crossover point was closer to the consonant release for the French group.

It is of course the bilinguals who are of interest in the present context. When they were producing French words in a French setting, the bilinguals (who had all learned French as their first language) matched the monolingual French group; there was no statistical difference between the two groups, and there was also no evidence of phonological interference from their second language, English. However, when they were producing English, their speech was not completely free of interference from French. This appeared, interestingly enough, in their production of voiced plosives rather than in their production of aspirated voiceless ones. The bilinguals had evidently learned to produce the aspiration in voiceless plosives, and they matched the performance of monolinguals in that respect. Initial voiced plosives are usually voiced for their whole duration in the speech of native speakers of French; what is phonemically a voiced plosive in English need not be so phonetically, and many speakers of English do not start voicing until immediately after the release of the plosive. The bilinguals carried over their French pronunciation habits into the production of English voiced plosives.

With respect to perception, the bilinguals appeared to make no distinction between the two languages: the crossover points for both curves were intermediate between the crossover points of the monolingual French and monolingual English speakers, and the two curves had similar shapes. The data thus show that language switching in bilinguals is well controlled for production but poorly controlled for perception at the phonological level.

Very similar results were obtained by Williams (1977) in her study of the perception of stop consonant voicing by Spanish-English bilinguals. She used eight bilingual subjects, who carried out labeling and discrimination tasks listening to stimuli taken from a synthetic speech continuum varying in voice onset time. Each subject also produced 16 examples of word-initial voiced and voiceless labial plosives in each language. The procedure was carried out in Spanish for one set of trials and in English for another set. The labeling performance of bilinguals was compared with that of Spanish and English monolinguals from a prior study (Williams 1974). The performance of the bilingual group on perception tasks differed from that of both monolingual groups; the bilinguals' production in their two languages conformed with results obtained from each monolingual group. Williams suggests that even though the bilingual may have the ability to distinguish perceptually the phonemic contrasts in both of his languages, he does not use the same acoustic properties as perceptual cues for a given contrast as does a monolingual speaker. Becoming bilingual may thus entail, among other things, a modification in the use of acoustic information present in the speech signal.

Elman, Diehl, and Buchwald (1977) criticize these two studies from the point of view of methodology. They focus on the fact that in the studies by Caramazza et al. and Williams the bilingual boundary did not differ according to the language used in conducting the session. Varying the language of the experimental instructions and of the pre-experimental conversation had no effect whatever on the placement of the voiced-voiceless boundary. Elman, Diehl, and Buchwald argue that the use of synthetic speech may have made it difficult to maintain a "language set." Furthermore, there had been a delay of several minutes between the set-inducing instructions and the actual presentation of the stimuli; there is some evidence from earlier studies that contextual effects diminish considerably when the interval is increased to 10 seconds and that they are virtually eliminated when this interval is filled with extraneous speech sounds.

The study of Elman, Diehl, and Buchwald was designed to provide a strong test of the hypothesis that the acoustic-to-phonemic mapping is unaffected by higher-order linguistic information and that bilinguals will therefore demonstrate fixed phoneme boundaries despite changes in language set. They used naturally produced test syllables; their test tapes included natural filler words along with the nonsense syllables, and each item was immediately preceded by a language-appropriate instruction to "write the word."

Two test tapes were prepared, each including exactly the same test syllables. On one of the tapes the filler words and the precursor sentences were in English; on the other the filler words and the precursors ("escriba la palabra") were in Spanish. All materials were spoken by the first author, who is a bilingual. Each tape contained 40 different filler words and 10 copies each of five different test syllables, all items being randomized. The five syllables had measured voice onset time values of -69, $+15$, $+19$, $+26$, and $+66$ msec. In a pilot study both monolingual English speakers and monolingual Spanish speakers uniformly identified the -69 msec stimulus as /b/ and the $+66$ msec stimulus as /p/. The three intermediate stimuli were ambiguous: English monolinguals heard them primarily as /b/, and Spanish monolinguals heard them primarily as /p/.

Three groups of subjects served in the experiment: 12 monolingual English speakers, who were presented with the English test tape; 11 monolingual Spanish speakers, who were presented with the Spanish test tape; and 31 English-Spanish bilinguals, who were presented with both tapes, on separate days.

The results were predictable for the two monolingual groups and for the two extreme stimuli for the bilingual group. Of interest were the responses of the bilinguals to the three ambiguous stimuli. As a group, these subjects reliably identified more of the test syllables as /ba/ when listening to the English tape than when listening to the Spanish tape. Furthermore, different degrees of bilingualism were reflected in the results. Of the 31 bilingual subjects, 15 were rated as strong bilinguals, 6 as moderate, and 10 as weak. The identification shift (as a function of linguistic set) was small and statistically insignificant for the moderate and weak bilingual subjects, whereas it was relatively large and significant for the strong bilinguals. The 5 subjects who received the highest bilingual rankings showed a very considerable shift, although their averages remained short of monolingual performance for either language.

The 2 most bilingual subjects demonstrated a virtually complete identification shift in two conditions. The remaining 13 strong bilinguals exhibited essentially monolingual performance in one of the two conditions; in the other language set, the phoneme boundary was shifted toward—but did not reach—the appropriate monolinguals' boundary location.

Elman, Diehl, and Buchwald did not test production; thus, their experiment does not furnish additional information about the bilinguals' ability to keep their two languages apart in production. The experiment does, however, provide strong support for the notion that for most bilinguals, the two languages interfere with each other in perception.

Grammatical Interference

Grammatical interference parallels phonic interference: interference takes place when elements of language B enter language A and are gradually grammatically integrated, or when a speaker of language A starts to speak language B and carries over elements of A into B. There are degrees of grammatical integration, just as there are degrees of phonic integration. We will consider both morphological interference and syntactic interference.

Interference is likely to take place when the two languages have different grammatical categories. In morphological integration, a word borrowed from language B into language A must be assigned grammatical categories that are characteristic of language A. Consider, for example, the grammatical category of gender associated with nouns. In a contact situation involving English on the one hand and Norwegian or German on the other hand, English nouns incorporated either into Norwegian or German must be assigned grammatical gender, since gender is an obligatory category in both languages. English lacks grammatical gender, although it possesses natural gender (it makes a distinction among masculine, feminine, and neuter in personal pronouns). Haugen (1969) discusses the process of gender assignment in American Norwegian. In the Norwegian spoken in Norway approximately 49.3% of all nouns are masculine, 24.0% are feminine, and 26.7% are neuter. In American Norwegian the feminine has virtually disappeared. All new nouns become masculine unless they are associated with a homophonous feminine or neuter morpheme or a female living being. Haugen believes that this technique of borrowing had already been established before emigration, in other words, that loanwords were normally made masculine. American Norwegian also shows a high degree of vacillation. In Haugen's study 18.7% of all noun stems showed more than one gender. By coincidence, this is the percentage of vacillation in the gender of English loanwords in standard German.

In Australian German, on the other hand, a "feminine tendency" prevails (Clyne 1972). Clyne attributes this to the similarity between the feminine definite article (*die*) in German and the accented form of the definite article in English. Thus, English loanwords entering Australian German became predominantly feminine: *die Buggy, die Fence, die Road, die Yard, die Car*. Similarities in meaning with corresponding German words account for some gender assignments: *das Breakfast* parallels *das Frühstück, die Gully* acquires its feminine gender from *die Schlucht*. Either the natural gender of living creatures or the parallel with German *der Hund* accounts for the masculine gender of *der Dog*.

Underdifferentiation appears when language B, which has gender distinctions, is used by a speaker of language A, which does not. It is well known to language teachers that students whose native language is English have difficulties in mastering the gender systems of languages like French and German. The problems of speakers of Finno-Ugric languages like Finnish and Estonian are compounded by the fact that these languages lack gender distinctions even in personal pronouns: Finnish *hän* and Estonian *tema* translate English *he, she,* and *it*. Frequently the use of the English (or German, or Russian) personal pronouns by speakers of these Finno-Ugric languages is more or less random; listeners ordinarily notice only those instances in which the pronoun is employed wrongly and may arrive at the impression that the speakers systematically reverse the pronouns and refer to males with a feminine pronoun and to females with a masculine pronoun.

In the process of grammatical integration each new word is given case endings according to the inflectional class to which it has been assigned. Degrees of integration may frequently be observed. For example, a number of French loanwords entered Russian in the nineteenth century, among them the word *paletot* 'overcoat' in the form *pal'to*. The French word is masculine; standard Russian dictionaries list *pal'to* as neuter. In standard usage the word is indeclinable; its neuter gender, however, represents assignment of the word to the large class of neuters ending in stressed -*o* in the nominative singular. I have been informed (personal communication by recent arrivals from Russia) that one now hears the plural form *pol'ta* in colloquial Russian: the morphological integration of the word is apparently complete, and the word is inflected in the same way as, for example, the native word *okno* 'window'.

In the integration of a loanword, plural suffixes are frequently treated as if they were part of the stem, and new plural markers are added: Norwegian *kars* – *karsar* 'cars', German *Keks* – *Kekse* 'cakes', Russian *rel's* – *rel'sy* 'rails', Estonian *props* – *propsid* 'pitprops'. On the other hand, an English final -*n* that is part of the stem may be treated as the postpositive definite article in Norwegian, and a back-formation may result: *pumpkin* enters American Norwegian as *panki*, with a definite form *pankin* and a newly formed plural *pankiar*.

Syntactic interference appears when patterns from language A are carried over into language B or when patterns of language B are interpreted in terms of patterns of language A. Interference between English and German word order, for example, is evident in constructions popularly associated with Pennsylvania German: *Throw mama from the train a kiss* or *Throw the baby from the window a cookie*. Relatively more subtle are differences in the ordering of verbal modifiers. In German an adverbial of time precedes an adverbial of place, whereas in English the order is reversed. The German sentence *Er kommt morgen nach Hause* may be turned by a speaker of German into the English sentence *He comes tomorrow home,* with the characteristic German ordering of modifiers and with clearly discernible interference.

Interference may also result in grammatical change within the borrowing language. An example might be the case of Yiddish *ver*, which has been identified with English *who*. Yiddish *ver* is an interrogative pronoun; English *who* has two functions, that of an interrogative pronoun and that of a relative pronoun. Through cross-language identification of these two morphemes, the functions of *ver* have been extended, and *ver* may now be likewise used as a relative pronoun.

An example of an experimental study of syntactic interference is provided by Lehiste (1971). This study attempted to establish the possible difference between native and nonnative speakers with respect to grammatical variability. A currently popular method of teaching elementary syntactic theory involves contrastive presentation of "grammatical" and "nongrammatical" sentences. There is increasing evidence, however, that native speakers do not necessarily agree among themselves about what is grammatical. A concrete problem arises in teaching a syntax course to a group of students including both native and nonnative speakers of the language from which the examples are drawn: nonnative speakers frequently fail to see the rationale for a particular decision concerning whether a sentence is or is not grammatical, if this rationale consists of an appeal to the native speaker's intuition, and if the native speakers do not agree among themselves.

The notion of grammaticality is difficult to define and even more difficult to explain to linguistically naive users of a language. One way to explore the reliability of native speakers' grammaticality judgments would be to compare the actual use of a grammatical feature by a group of monolingual native speakers of English with the use of the same feature by a group of bilinguals for whom English is a second language. The grammatical feature selected for my 1971 study was the formation of tag questions. Langendoen (1970) had presented a set of 91 English sentences to a group of 46 English teachers, all of whom were native speakers of English. I presented the same sentences to a comparable group of 46 Estonian-English bilinguals. The selected feature is very suitable for testing with this group, since Es-

Concept of Interference 17

tonian does not know tag questions of the English kind; a statement might be turned into a question by the use of a phrase similar to the German *nicht wahr* or the French *n'est-ce pas*, but even that would not be very common. The educational level of the two groups was comparable, and all bilinguals had had some formal instruction in English grammar, although they were not as familiar with formalized "school grammar" as the monolingual group consisting of teachers of the English language.

In order to establish some measure of the degree of similarity between the two groups, I defined the notion of "deviant response" as a variant of a tag question not included among the set of variants offered by the members of the monolingual group in response to a specific sentence calling for confirmation. A gross comparison of the two sets of 4,186 tag questions yielded 701 deviant responses on the part of the bilinguals, amounting to 16.7% of the total. A separate analysis of the deviant responses of each bilingual subject showed that the number of deviant responses ranged from 1 to 68 (out of 91). Almost half of the deviant responses were furnished by six individuals. The other subjects averaged fewer than 10 deviant responses each. Furthermore, many of the apparent deviations seemed to have no linguistic significance. The monolingual group, being English teachers, had a clear notion of what a tag question is; the bilingual group seemed to have considerable difficulty in grasping what was required of them, and many of their responses suggest that they must have thought they were participating in a free association test. There was also considerable variability among the monolingual subjects: the number of different tag questions formed in response to a sentence ranged from 1 to 8. The bilinguals showed somewhat greater grammatical variability: the number of their responses to one and the same sentence ranged between 2 and 13. If the six individuals who contributed half of the deviant responses were excluded, the difference between the monolinguals and the bilinguals appeared quite small. There were two types of deviant responses that might be considered indicative of interference from Estonian: 5 responses that seem to translate the Estonian equivalent of *nicht wahr* and *n'est-ce pas*, and 27 pronoun references in which *he* was used for *she* and vice versa. (As noted, Estonian has no grammatical gender and has only one form for the third person pronoun.)

The systematic study of the transfer of elements from language A to language B, when the speaker of A attempts to produce B, is called *contrastive analysis*. The basic assumption of contrastive analysis is that by contrasting the structures of the "source language" (A) and the "target language" (B), one will be able to predict the errors made by learners of the target language, and it will therefore be possible to design teaching materials to take account of the anticipated errors. Mackey (1965) formulated this assumption as follows:

Differential description is of particular interest to language teaching because many of the difficulties in learning a second language are due to the fact that it differs from the first. So that if we subtract the characteristics of the first language from those of the second, what presumably remains is a list of the learner's difficulties.

Complementary to contrastive analysis is error analysis. It should be kept in mind that there are at least two kinds of errors: errors due to interference, and errors due to mistaken generalization of an incompletely learned rule. Errors of the second kind might be made by children learning the language as a first (native) language, whereas errors of the first kind are typical mistakes made by foreigners (although adult learners, too, may commit errors of the second kind).

A series of projects in contrastive analysis has been carried out over the past 20 years. Below are some examples of problems that have been encountered by scholars working on the Yugoslav Serbocroatian-English Contrastive Project between 1967 and 1980 (see Filipović 1975, 1982).

Contrastive analysis predicts that one trouble spot encountered by speakers of one language in learning the other will be demonstratives: English has two forms (*this* and *that*), whereas Serbocroatian has three (*ovaj*, *onaj*, and *taj*). *Ovaj* refers to (masculine) objects that are close both to the speaker and to the interlocutor; *onaj* is remote from

Concept of Interference

both; and *taj* is remote from the speaker but close to the interlocutor. *Taj* thus translates into English both as *this* and as *that*. Interference may be expected in the use of *taj* by speakers of English and in the use of *this* and *that* by speakers of Serbocroatian. A detailed study was made of the equivalences and mistakes made by both groups of speakers, and a test was devised that can be employed in teaching the proper usage of *this* and *that* to speakers of Serbocroatian. The test consists of checking possible alternations in Serbocroatian: *taj* will have *this* as its English equivalent when it can alternate with *ovaj*, and *that* when it cannot.

A speaker of Serbocroatian produced the following English sentence: *The government was in Austria and in* this *time Maribor was called Marburg*. The common Serbocroatian expression, which the speaker apparently had in mind, is *u to vreme* 'at that time' (*to* is the neuter form of *taj*). In this expression *to* can alternate with the neuter form of *onaj* but not with *ovaj: u ono vreme* would be acceptable, but *u ovo vreme* would not. Correct English usage can be taught by asking the Serbocroatian speakers to test whether the form of *taj* may or may not alternate with a form of *ovaj*. Contrastive analysis correctly predicted the difficulty, and error analysis suggests a pedagogical solution.

Lexical Interference

Lexical interference may result from contact between the vocabularies of two languages. There are various ways in which the vocabulary of one language can interfere with that of another. The introduction of a new word to designate a new concept enlarges the vocabulary and frequently affects the niches occupied by existing words in the broader semantic field to which the new word constitutes a contribution. Some examples of *simple morpheme transfer* into English might be the following: *czar* 'autocratic all-powerful ruler' from Russian, *quisling* 'collaborator with an occupying enemy power' from the Norwegian name Quisling, *coolie* 'laborer performing extremely hard physical work under conditions of exploitation' from Hindi, *mafioso* 'member of a group engaged in organized crime' from Italian, *sputnik* 'artificial satellite' from Russian, and *kindergarten* 'preschool organized activity for children' from German.

The term *loanshift* is applied to cases in which the meaning of a morpheme in language A is modified or changed on the model of language B. Typical examples of extension of meaning of a morpheme in language A to include the meaning of the same morpheme in language B are the following (Haugen 1950). In Colorado Spanish the word *ministro* 'cabinet member' now also designates a Protestant clergyman, on the model of English *minister*. The German verb *nachschauen* 'to look after' originally applied to a concrete situation; now it has acquired the additional meaning 'to take care of' on the model of the English phrase 'to look after', which has both a concrete and a metaphoric meaning. The German verb *treiben* 'to drive' can now be used to refer to driving a car (*einen Wagen treiben*)—clearly an extension of the original meaning on the basis of the broader meaning of the equivalent English morpheme.

The preceding examples (which could be easily multiplied) constitute instances in which the shift in meaning resulted in an extension. A complete change of meaning, a semantic shift, results from the introduction of loan homonyms. In such cases the new meaning has nothing in common with the old meaning. Thus, *grosseria* in American Portuguese has changed its meaning from 'rude remark' to 'grocery store'; *korn* in American Norwegian now means 'maize' instead of 'grain': *livraria* in American Portuguese means 'library' rather than 'bookstore' (the original Portuguese word for 'library' is *biblioteca*).

An extremely common form of lexical interference is the *loan translation* or *calque*. Examples can be found in practically every language. Thus Latin *impressio* has been translated into German as *Eindruck* and *expressio* as *Ausdruck* (English has resorted to outright borrowing); Latin *paeninsula* has become French *presqu'île*, German *Kindergarten* has yielded Russian *detskij sad*. Sometimes the model is borrowed rather than the exact morphemes: English *skyscraper* has yielded German *Wolkenkratzer*, which would literally translate a non-existent English word *cloudscratcher*. *Blends* and *hybrids* arise when several processes apply at the same time: a loan morpheme may be filled into native models, one element of a compound may be imported, and so on. Thus, *ground floor* appears in Pennsylvania German as *Grundfloor*, and *plum pie* becomes *Blaumepai*. Loan translations and hybrids are frequently found in proper names and geographical names: *New York* becomes *Neuyork* in German, Afrikaans *Kaapstad* appears in German as *Kapstadt* and in English as *Cape Town;* practically every seagoing nation refers to the *Cape of Good Hope* by a loan translation (for example, German *Das Kap der Guten Hoffnung,* Estonian *Hea Lootuse neem*); the Italian name *Giovanni* is changed to *John* when the Pope bearing the name is referred to in English-language newspapers.

Loanwords experience phonological and morphological/grammatical integration; at the same time they are gradually integrated into the lexicon. A new word may simply be added to the vocabulary (simple morpheme transfer), especially if it designates a new item or concept. More frequently, however, the lexicon already contains another word with a more or less closely related meaning. It seems that for a while both words may be used side by side until the old word is discarded or the two words become specialized. Old words may, of course, be dropped from the lexicon without language contact—sometimes without any apparent reason, at other times as a result of cultural change (for example, the technical terminology of hand weaving may disappear when the techniques are forgotten). Thus, all Romance languages inherited from Latin the word *bellum* 'war'; French has substituted for it the word *guerre*, which is of Frankish origin. No semantic change seems to be involved, and the original word has simply been discarded.

When the old word continues to exist side by side with the new one, the lexicon is frequently restructured. The meaning of the old word may become specialized. The Estonian word *pii* 'tooth' belongs to the inherited Finno-Ugric layer of the lexicon; *hammas* 'tooth' is a Baltic loanword. As a result of the introduction of *hammas, pii* now refers only to the teeth of a comb or the teeth of a rake; the use of *hammas* in these contexts would be impossible. Or the two words may acquire stylistic differences. Thus, many Norman French loanwords in English carry a bookish or "high style" connotation, whereas corresponding Anglo-Saxon stems are either neutral or "low style." Compare the shades of meaning associated with word pairs like *read–peruse, buy–purchase,* and *sweat–perspiration.*

Borrowed words are most frequently nouns, verbs, or adjectives. Bound morphemes, such as derivative suffixes, are borrowed only rarely, since bound morphemes usually indicate grammatical categories, and interference hardly ever results in the addition of new categories to a language. New phonemes are hardly ever borrowed either, but an allophone may become a phoneme as a result of the influx of loanwords. Integration of loanwords into the lexicon usually just adds new members to old categories. In the rare cases in which bound morphemes are borrowed, we are dealing with instances of intimate contact between two languages that must have lasted for a considerable time. The contact between Anglo-Saxon and Norman French appears to have been of that type, and English has acquired some productive derivative suffixes. As long as the suffix *-able, -ible* appears only with Romance stems, we cannot confidently claim that it is the suffix that has been borrowed; but the lexicon now contains such pairs as *legible–readable, edible–eatable,* and new creations like *get-at-able*—ample evidence that the borrowed suffix has become productive.

Lexical interference can be studied systematically in various ways. Investigation of *code switching* can provide some interesting information concerning the ways in which a bilingual handles the vocabularies of his two languages.

We have defined code switching as the alternate use of two languages by the same speaker during the same speech event. According to Weinreich (1953), the ideal bilingual controls his choice of language rigidly, switching according to interlocutor and topic but "certainly not within a single sentence" (p. 73). Haugen (1956) postulated three stages of linguistic diffusion: switching, interference, and integration. The question is now whether the first stage, switching, occurs at random or follows some identifiable pattern, and whether it is possible to pinpoint some factors that may cause the bilingual to perform the switch. Up to now we have concentrated on what happens to the language in a contact situation; when we start looking for reasons for code switching, we shift our primary attention to the bilingual individual.

The speech of Spanish-English bilinguals in the American Southwest has been studied extensively over a period of time (Hernandez-Chavez, Cohen, and Beltramo 1975); Different opinions have been expressed regarding the switching that occurs in their speech. For example, Espinosa (1957) described switching as random intermingling of Spanish and English words. Gumperz and Hernandez (1971) saw a direct functional similarity between code switching on the one hand and style switching within a single language on the other. Very subtle social and psychological factors operate in code switching where the interlocutor and situation are held constant.

Lance (1969) demonstrated that code switching between English and Spanish is not entirely random, but that certain kinds of lexical items are more susceptible to switching than others. He claimed that language switching does not occur simply because the speaker does not know a particular word in one language or the other; rather, the word or phrase that is most readily available at the moment for some reason is the one that comes out. The task of the investigator is to determine the reasons why a particular word or phrase is more readily available.

Lance's research team interviewed three generations of a bilingual family in Bryan, Texas, in order to study their usage of English and Spanish. The abundant material collected and analyzed by the team provides illustrations for many kinds of switching between the two languages, for example, insertion of single words or terms into a sentence, insertion of longer phrases or clauses, and quotations involving Spanish introductions to English quotations with switching within them. Introduction of English words into otherwise Spanish sentences appeared to be triggered by quasi-technical terminology—words that have specialized uses in American culture or technology. Many words were adapted morphologically, but others were simply transferred, such as *troca*–'truck', *diche*–'ditch', *pompa*–'pump', *paipa*–'pipe', *queque*–'cake'. Some of the words were phonologically adapted, some were not. Spanish words used in English sentences were limited largely to such terms as *tortilla, enchilada,* and *taco,* for which there are no equivalent English terms. The speakers occasionally pronounced these words with some English phonology (for instance, with a retroflex *r* and a final schwa in *tortilla* and with a slightly aspirated *t* in *taco*).

Many of the switches into English in the midst of otherwise Spanish sentences seemed to be related to the fact that certain terms are used most often in situations that call for English. Numbers were given in English when naming street addresses and prices but in Spanish when referring to the number of children in a family. Thus, sentences like the following might be produced (Lance 1975:139): *Vivo 'horita en siete . . . seven hundred por la Lucky Street* 'I am living now at 700 Lucky Street'. In a number of instances the use of one or the other language seemed to reflect the speaker's (possibly subconscious) assessment of the range of his auditors' lexicons.

Lance found examples of switching in so many grammatical environments that he concluded that there are no syntactic restrictions on where the switching can occur. Gumperz and Hernandez (1971), on the other hand, did find some restrictions, though they admit that the extent of these restrictions is not known.

In his study of Australian German, Clyne (1972) identified several kinds of trigger words (words that apparently facilitate switching between the two languages). Especially common was switching connected with homophonous diamorphs such as the preposition *in*, which has the same form and meaning in both languages. Examples given by Clyne include *Bäume am Hang mit Häuser in between* 'Trees on the hillside with houses in between' and *Das ist das Cafe near dem Oriental Restaurant* 'That is the cafe near the Oriental Restaurant'. Proper names and loanwords also triggered switching. Anticipational switching occurred frequently at the beginning of a prepositional phrase, a noun phrase, and a clause.

What does the extensive switching in the speech of bilinguals say about their linguistic competence? Are they aware of the switching, and are they aware of different degrees and kinds of "foreign" elements in one of their languages?

These questions were addressed by Beltramo and de Porcel (1975) in a study involving Spanish-English bilinguals. In this study 50 bilinguals were asked to classify loanwords in 60 Spanish sentences. Of these sentences, 40 contained loanwords, one per sentence; 20 were without English loanwords; and 10 contained words having cognates in English with a different meaning (the assumption being that these might be felt to be "less Spanish" than words that had no cognates). The subjects' task was to identify the words on a scale involving five steps: Pure Spanish, Almost Spanish, Half and Half, Almost English, and Definitely English. Pure Spanish included two subcategories: "A cognate, but used correctly in Spanish" and "Acceptable Spanish." "Almost Spanish" included loan translations and loanshift extensions: familiar Spanish words in new environments. "Half and Half" designated morphologically adapted words with English stems; it was assumed that such words should be felt as closer to English than to Spanish. When both morphological and phonological adaptation was present, the word was classified as "Almost English"; when the only adaptation was phonological, the word was classified as "Definitely English." Ten points was the possible score in each category. Examples of the different types of test sentences containing loanwords are given below.

Este highway es muy peligroso 'This highway is very dangerous' (English word)

Dicen que Jose va a cuitear su trabajo 'They say that Jose is going to quit his job' (Part English, part Spanish)
Su hijo va a la escuela alta 'His son goes to high school' (Loan translation)
¿Tienen Ustedes unas questiones? 'Do you have any questions?' (Loanshift)
Elena es muy sensible a los cambios de clima 'Helen is very sensitive to changes of climate' (Cognate, but used correctly in Spanish).

Beltramo and de Porcel were concerned with both sociological variables (such as degree of acculturation) and linguistic variables. It turned out that higher acculturation was associated with higher scores on the loanword test only in a single category: phonological adaptation. The subject group as a whole revealed a striking consistency in the relative sensitivity to English in each of the loan types. Mean scores for the six types were as follows (that is, average number of correct responses out of a possible score of ten):

Phonological adaptation (Definitely English)	6.58
Morphological adaptation (Almost English)	4.28
Loan translation	3.54
Loanshift	2.96
Spanish with cognates	7.60
Spanish without cognates	8.86

A statistical analysis of the results makes it possible to draw the following conclusions. Native words, and English words transferred to Spanish by mere phonological adaptation, were indeed more easily recognized with respect to English influence than the more "mixed" types. Pure native words (with and without English cognates) were significantly more easily recognized as Spanish than phonologically adapted borrowings were recognized as English. The existence of cognates in English interfered significantly with the recognition of native words as "Pure Spanish." Within "mixed" types an English influence involving form and meaning was more easily recognized as

English than an influence affecting meaning only. There was no significant difference between loanshifts and loan translations.

The study revealed clearly that bilinguals are aware of the interference (English influence in this case) and that the degrees of interference depended on linguistic factors rather than social ones: regardless of how much the bilinguals differed in their use of Spanish, or in age, education, or other social variables that may reflect acculturation to the larger society, their bilingual competence was about the same as far as their awareness of English influence in the lexicon was concerned.

One result is particularly significant: the finding that knowledge of English (awareness of the existence of English cognates) interfered with the recognition of a purely Spanish word as being purely Spanish. This has implications for the question whether a bilingual has two separate linguistic systems or some combination of the two, a question we will consider at greater length in the next chapter.

Recommended Reading

Haugen, E. (1969). *The Norwegian Language in America: A Study in Bilingual Behavior.* Bloomington, Ind.: Indiana University Press.

Hernandez-Chavez, E., A. D. Cohen, and A. F. Beltramo, eds. (1975). *El Lenguaje de los Chicanos: Regional and Social Characteristics Used by Mexican-Americans.* Arlington, Va.: Center for Applied Linguistics.

Weinreich, U. (1953). *Languages in Contact.* New York: Linguistic Circle of New York.

Whiteley, W. H., ed. (1971). *Language Use and Social Change.* London: Oxford University Press.

Chapter 2
Bilingualism: The Bilingual Individual

Both Uriel Weinreich and Einar Haugen have emphasized the crucial role of the bilingual individual in language contact. Weinreich said, "The locus of language contact is in the mind of the bilingual"; Haugen observed, "The locus of bilingualism is in the individual mind." Obviously it is not languages that enter into contact, but speakers; and thus it is natural that the speaker who uses more than one language becomes the focus of interest in the study of language contact.

The basic questions that arise in this connection concern the ways in which bilinguals differ from monolinguals and the possible differences among various kinds of bilinguals. We have observed examples of interference working in both directions: ways in which knowledge of the first language interferes with the second language, and ways in which knowledge of the second language interferes with the first. Transfer of elements from the first language into the second is common at all levels, starting with "foreign accent" and ending with loanshift extensions and loan translations. Less easily observed is the influence of the second language on the first; we have, however, considered some phonological examples (the perception of voice onset time by English-French and English-Spanish bilinguals), as well as some lexical-semantic examples (the experiment with Spanish words that did or did not have cognates in English, in which bilinguals perceived words with English cognates as being significantly "less Spanish"). Monolinguals differ from these bilinguals in a trivial way by

The Bilingual Individual

simply not being subject to these kinds of interference. But they differ in other ways as well, and scholars have developed several research techniques for investigating this subject. We shall briefly review some of these studies, starting with those that explore the nature of the bilingual lexicon.

Ervin and Osgood (1954) distinguished between two types of bilingual individuals, the coordinate and the compound. Coordinate bilinguals have learned their two languages in separate settings; compound bilinguals have acquired them in the same setting and use them interchangeably. *Coordinate bilinguals* have learned the two languages with disassociated meanings for parallel signs; *compound bilinguals* have mastered their two languages in such a way that the equivalent words of each language are linked to one meaning. It is known that the majority of right-handed monolinguals have a language center in the left hemisphere of the brain; one question that might be asked concerns the location of the language center of the bilingual. Are the two languages stored at the same location or at separate locations? Is there a difference in the way the lexicon is stored between monolinguals and bilinguals on the one hand, and between coordinate and compound bilinguals on the other hand? Are the lexical storage systems of the two languages of the bilingual independent or interdependent, and is that related to whether the speaker is a coordinate or a compound bilingual? Is the degree of independence related to the difference between linguistic systems—for example, do we find more overlap between the lexicons if the languages share numerous cognates and use the same writing system (as do English and German), as compared to languages with few cognates and differing writing systems (such as English and Chinese)?

Many of these questions have been treated by Albert and Obler (1978), who also review a large number of previous studies. We will restrict ourselves to a representative sample.

Three techniques have been employed in the study of the bilingual's lexical storage systems: word association tasks, list-learning tasks, and studies of semantic measures. In association studies the subject is asked to produce the first word that comes to mind after the presentation of a stimulus word. The associations may be free or restricted; the stimuli may be from only one language or from both languages; and so on.

One fairly obvious result of association studies is the finding that greater proficiency in a language results in more associations. Thus, in a study by Riegel and Zivian (1972), 24 English-dominant English-German bilinguals were asked to write as many words as they could in three minutes; they produced an average of 66 words in English and 31 in German. The manner of acquisition of the second language appears to have an influence on the choice of response: persons who have learned the second language in a different cultural setting tend to give more diverse responses, whereas persons who have learned the second language in a school setting tend to give translation equivalents. Rūķe-Draviņa (1971) analyzed the kinds of responses given by three groups of subjects to four Swedish words. The three groups consisted of adult Swedish speakers, adult Latvian speakers, and young Swedish-Latvian bilinguals who had grown up in Sweden. The two adult groups contained subjects who were familiar with several other languages, even though they spoke only their mother tongue fluently; the adults had grown up in different cultural settings, whereas the young bilinguals had grown up in a Swedish cultural setting.

The four stimulus words consisted of one noun, two adjectives, and one verb. The adjectives were color adjectives, /RED/ and /WHITE/ (Swedish *röd* and *vit,* Latvian *sarkans* and *balts*). The test verb /TO WORK/ and the test noun /WORK/ were derived from the same stem in Swedish (*arbeta* and *arbete*) but from different stems in Latvian (*stradat* and *darbs*). There were 13 subjects in the Swedish group, 16 in the Latvian group, and 11 in the young bilingual group. All test words were presented in Swedish, orally as well as in writing, to the Swedish group, and in Latvian to the other two groups. The subjects had five minutes in which to write down all words that came to mind after the presentation of the test word, regardless of language.

The Bilingual Individual

The test revealed some differences among the three groups. The differences are connected with several factors, some linguistic, some related to personal experience. Thus, subjects in the Swedish group mentioned words from some semantic fields that never appeared among the responses of the Latvian group; words belonging to the same semantic field and appearing among the responses of both groups could vary in frequency between the two groups; and there were differences in the emotional undertone of associations with a given word.

The stimulus word /RED/ received a large number of responses signifying /HOUSE/, /CABIN/, /BUILDING/ from Swedish subjects; no Latvian subject associated /RED/ with a word signifying a building. The author suggests the explanation that red houses and cottages are not common in Latvia, whereas they are characteristic of Sweden. Two of the young bilinguals gave responses of this kind, and their responses were in Swedish (to a Latvian stimulus); the association appears clearly connected with the Swedish environment in which the young bilinguals had grown up.

On the other hand, the two adult groups differed from the young bilinguals in their associations with the words /TO WORK/ and /WORK/: the predominant associations of the young bilingual group were with /MONEY/, /PAY/, /SALARY/, whereas the two adult groups mentioned notions of /DUTY/ and /PLEASURE/ at least as often as /MONEY/. In general, the positive emotional attitude toward /WORK/ was outstanding for the Latvian adult group, somewhat weaker for the Swedish adult group, and completely absent from the young bilingual group. Language differences seemed to play a negligible role compared to differences in generation. The Swedish group's most frequent response to the stimulus *arbeta* 'to work' turned out to be /TO TAKE A JOB/ and /TO EXERT ONESELF/, whereas the Latvian group's most frequent response was /TIRED/.

A detailed analysis of the sequences of associations showed that subjects tended to be influenced by the phonemic and morphemic structure of the stimulus word (or the preceding word in the association chain). The phonemic similarity between the beginnings of words appeared to stimulate the associating process. For instance, the following association chain was produced in response to Latvian *darbs* 'work' (noun): (Latvian) *darbs un maize* 'work and bread', (Latvian) *tautas darbinieki* 'men in public life', (Latvian) *darbs dara daritaju* 'practice makes perfect', (German) *darben* 'to suffer privations', (German) *verderben* 'to spoil, to ruin', (Latvian) *dargs* 'dear, expensive'. This sequence also illustrates the tendency to produce clusters of words in each language, when subjects are free to alternate between languages in chain association.

Influence of the morphemic structure of words became apparent in sequences of derivatives with the same suffix or compounds built in the same way: for instance, Swedish *förvandling* 'transformation', *omdaning* 'remaking', *omvälvning* 'razing', or *oskuld* 'innocent', *oskriven* 'unwritten', *okänd* 'unknown'.

As noted, subjects frequently switched between languages; as individuals with higher education, they had some acquaintance with a number of languages, and response words appeared in nine of them. Response words in a language other than that of the stimulus word were given by members of all three groups. In the monolingual group these words were, as a rule, translations of the stimulus word or of the preceding word in the association chain. The typical bilingual or multilingual participants, on the other hand, continued the association chain while switching from one language into another. A new idea, semantically connected with the previous concepts, could be expressed in another linguistic code. The switching appeared to be facilitated by interlingual homonyms. (This confirms the previously noted observations of M. G. Clyne with regard to homophonous diamorphs.) Rapid switches between languages were particularly characteristic of multilinguals. Since the frequent language switching involved true chaining of association, it may be concluded that the subjects possessed a unified cognition system, with output possible in any language.

It should be kept in mind that Rūķe-Draviņa's monolinguals were in many respects similar to compound bilinguals, who had been exposed to several languages in school but within the same cultural setting.

Lexical organization can also be studied by the technique of list learning and list recall. In studies of this type subjects are presented with lists of words and are asked to recall as many of them as possible after the stimulus list has been withdrawn. The lists can be mixed or monolingual; the items can be related semantically; the presentation can be visual or auditory; the interval between presentations can be varied and can be filled (or not filled) with potentially interfering tasks. The comparison of mixed-language lists and same-language lists, for example, can provide information about the degree of independence or interdependence of the bilingual's lexical systems.

Lambert, Havelka, and Crosby (1958) designed an experiment to refine the notions of compound and coordinate bilingualism. Their subjects were 32 balanced French-English bilinguals; half had acquired their two languages in a fused situation where both languages could be used interchangeably (compound bilinguals), and half with a certain degree of separation between appropriate usage situations (coordinate bilinguals). The coordinate bilinguals were further divided into unicultural and bicultural groups (unicultural–one parent used each language, or one language was used at home and one at school; bicultural–the two languages were learned in two cultural contexts). The subjects were presented with a list of 20 English words to be recalled; between the presentation and the recall the subjects were presented with another list, which was either a list of nonsense words or a list of French words. For the compound group, the French list facilitated the recall of English words; there was no difference between the French list and the nonsense list for the two kinds of coordinate bilinguals.

Kolers (1965) studied the difference between linguistic coding and coding based on some arbitrary principle. He argued that language is a coding system for its speakers; it consists of categories (words) and the rules for joining them intelligibly. A well-learned linguistic system would have different functional properties from some more arbitrary code. This should have an effect on short-term memory: the number of words a bilingual can recall from an unconnected list should be greater when he can use a well-formed coding system than when he must use an arbitrary one.

Kolers used 16 bilingual subjects, half native speakers of English who had lived in France for at least one year, and half native speakers of French who had lived in the United States for at least one year. The test material consisted of eight sets of nouns, each set consisting of three 70-word lists. Four of these were distributed in a color category, and four in a language category. The color category words were English monosyllables printed in red or black; the language category words were English or French monosyllables. In the first set in the color category the words appeared only in red; in the second set they appeared only in black; in the third set half appeared in red and half in black; and in the fourth set each word appeared both in red and in black. The first two sets were called "unicodal," the third "mixed," and the fourth "doubled." The language category words were grouped in a similar way. The first set was in English; the second was in French; the third consisted of the same number of words in English and French, but without translation; and the fourth contained every word and its translation. The first two sets were called "unilingual," the third "mixed," and the fourth "doubled."

The words were presented on a memory drum, one word per second, with an interval of 15 seconds between the lists. The subjects observed the whole list and then had two minutes to write down all the words they remembered from the list. When responding in the color category, the subjects wrote their responses in red or black ink; when responding in the language category, they wrote in French or English. The first 10 and the last 10 words were omitted from the analysis, so that it concerned the 50 interior words. The average number of interior words recalled from the unicodal lists did not differ from the average number of words recalled from the unilingual lists. However, the subjects recalled twice as many words from the mixed language lists as they recalled from the mixed color lists. The average number of words recalled from each set of lists was as follows: Black, 11.05; Red, 11.5; Mixed Color, 5.7; Doubled Color, 5.8; English, 9.1; French, 13.8; Mixed Language, 12.6; Doubled Language, 8.5.

Kolers interprets the results on the basis of the difference between the kinds of coding involved in language lists and color lists. Bilingual subjects have well-formed rules that define set membership of the individual words; they have no need to remember them actively as paired items. In recalling words from the color lists, they must engage in paired-associates learning; that is, they must remember both the word and its color. It is simply easier for them to remember whether the word was French of English than whether it was red or black. An interesting additional finding in this study is the lack of significant difference between mixed and doubled lists. Albert and Obler (1978) suggest that lexical storage for the two languages was separate enough that the translation equivalent of an item provided no more interference than any other word.

Kolers (1968) reported on another recall task that gave evidence for language interdependence in the bilingual. He used French-English subjects who were presented visually with a mixed language list of words. Some of the words were repeated more than once in the same language; other words were repeated in the other language (that is, the list contained both a word and its translation equivalent). These words were chosen in such a way that the word itself and its translation equivalent shared no visual or phonetic elements (for instance, *pli–fold*). Kolers found that the two kinds of repetition facilitated recall equally and concluded that the subjects were storing items semantically.

The same conclusion emerged from a study by Evers (1970). Evers's subjects were 40 bilingual college students in the United States, half native speakers of English and half native speakers of German. The presentation was auditory rather than visual: the subjects listened to taped lists of common monosyllabic and disyllabic nouns and were asked to recall orally as many of them as possible. Some tapes included translation equivalent pairs; those were found to facilitate recall. There were also numerous recall errors involving the wrong language. Evers concluded that a bilingual stores auditorily presented items in terms of underlying semantic concepts and has difficulty noting the language tag of the item, even when specifically requested to do so.

The list-learning studies, of which only a few have been reviewed, generally support the idea that lexical storage in the bilingual is to a certain degree interdependent. There is no doubt that a word and its translation equivalent are connected in a nonrandom way. Thus, the study of Evers (1970) showed that the inclusion of translation equivalents facilitated recall. It frequently happened that the language tag was forgotten, whereas the concept designated by the word was remembered. There was also some evidence for interference: in general, unilingual lists were recalled better than mixed lists. Albert and Obler (1978) suggest that this might be due to the fact that unilingual lists contained items in a single category, and categorized lists are generally recalled better than uncategorized ones.

Lexicosemantic tests involve manipulation of semantic processing. For example, such a test may compare the relative difficulty of divorcing lexical form from lexical content in each language of a bilingual. If different semantic processing skills are found in the two languages, tentative conclusions may be drawn about possible linguistic or cognitive differences between the bilingual's two languages.

Lambert, Havelka, and Crosby (1958) tried to elucidate differences between compound and coordinate bilinguals by employing, among others, a test of semantic satiation. The technique involved presenting the subjects with a word and asking them to place it on a semantic scale. Thus, the word *house* would be rated on a scale ranging from *good* to *bad*, and the word *maison* would be placed on a scale ranging from *bon* to *mauvais*. Coordinate subjects with bicultural experience were found to respond differently to translation equivalent items on the same dimension; for example, the word *house* might be rated fairly *good*, whereas the word *maison* might be rated more *mauvais*.

There was no difference between compound bilinguals on the one hand and coordinate bilinguals without real experience in two cultures on the other hand. This study revealed the interdependence of the two lexicons for compound bilinguals and essentially monocultural coordinates, and relatively greater independence of the two systems for bicultural coordinate bilinguals.

There is some evidence that bilinguals treat language more abstractly than do monolinguals. A famous study by Leopold (1939–49) showed that bilingual children achieve linguistic relativity (here, the ability to separate the phonetic shape of words from their meanings) at an earlier stage than monolingual children. Ianco-Worrall (1972) designed several experiments to test Leopold's observations. Her subjects were 30 Afrikaans-English bilingual children in two age groups, 4–6 years and 7–9 years old. Each bilingual child was paired with two unilingual children, one speaking Afrikaans, the other English; the children were matched for intelligence, age, sex, school grade, and social class. Bilingualism was defined as dual acquisition of language in a one-person, one-language home environment, in circumstances similar to those described by Leopold.

Attention to meaning or to sound of words was tested with the semantic and phonetic preference test, consisting of eight verbally presented, one-syllable sets of words. Each set consisted of three words: the standard word, a choice word phonetically related to the standard word, and a choice word semantically related to the standard word. The subject was told, "I have three words: *cap, can,* and *hat.* Which is more like *cap, can* or *hat*?" Exploratory studies have shown that on this test, semantic preference increases with age. A subject who chose the semantic item on at least 66% of the trials was judged to be using semantic criteria, and a subject who chose the phonetic item on 66% of the trials was judged to be using phonetic criteria.

The results showed that of the 4–6-year-old bilinguals, 54% consistently chose to interpret similarity between words in terms of the semantic dimension; of the unilingual groups of the same age, not a single Afrikaans speaker and only one English speaker showed similar behavior. Unilinguals showed increase of semantic preference as a function of age and arrived at comparable levels in the 7–9-year-old group. Ianco-Worrall draws the conclusion that bilinguals reach a stage in semantic development some two to three years earlier than their unilingual peers: the bilinguals make an earlier division of semantic and phonological properties than monolinguals.

Two independent tests of cognitive functioning were performed on the same subjects, which showed no developmental differences between the bilingual and monolingual subjects. Thus, bilingualism does not necessarily change cognitive abilities in general, even though it may induce earlier or better abilities to deal with language abstractly. It is important to note that bilingualism does not impede cognitive development either, in spite of widespread popular misconceptions to that effect.

Lexical units are relatively easy to define and test, and the majority of psychological studies of the language characteristics of bilinguals has focused on them. It is relatively more difficult to design experiments for studying bilingual sentence processing. We shall review just one such study, devoted to the retention of semantic, syntactic, and language information by young bilingual children (Heras and Nelson 1972). The authors based their study on the findings of Sachs (1967), who provided evidence that adults code sentences in terms of meaning, quickly forgetting syntactical details once the meaning of the sentence has been derived. An adaptation of Sachs's technique was used to assess syntactic and semantic coding by bilingual 5-year-olds; the authors examined in addition the possible coding in terms of the language in which a sentence was presented. The subjects were 20 children between 4.5 and 5.5 years of age, bilingual in English and Spanish. The test materials consisted of three-sentence stories; in each story two of the sentences were in one language and one was in the other language. Immediately after reading a story, the experimenter read a test sentence and asked the child (in the same language as the test sentence) whether the test sentence had occurred in the story. For eight of the stories, the test sentence was identical in meaning and syntax with the story's second sentence; for the remaining stories, the test sentence was either changed in syntax but not meaning or changed in meaning but not syntax. For each story, the subject was also asked whether the last (third) sentence in the story was presented in English or in Spanish; the question was posed in the same language as the recognition test that preceded the question about the language of the third sentence.

The subjects were much more successful in detecting semantic change than in detecting syntactic change: the number of correct responses per recognition test averaged .825 for semantically changed sentences but only .363 for syntactically changed sentences. Sentences that had in fact been syntactically changed were judged as unchanged 64% of the time. The simplest interpretation of these results is that the children derived the meaning of the original sentence and then rapidly forgot its syntactic details. This finding parallels those of Sachs (1967). With respect to language tagging, the children were more successful in identifying the language of presentation when the sentence and the interpolated material (the recognition test) were in the same language (mean = .700) than when the sentence and the interpolated material were in different languages (mean = .531); in the latter case identification was close to chance level. This observation, too, suggests that surface details of the sentence could be lost relatively easily. Heras and Nelson conclude that sentence meaning was coded, and retained successfully, in a way that did not depend upon original syntactic form or original language.

The psychological studies just reviewed suggest that bilingual subjects process language at some semantic level that is not totally dependent on the language in which the meaning is encoded. The lexicons of the two languages seem more or less compounded, depending to a certain extent on the manner in which and/or the age at which the two languages were acquired. The systems of production and perception appear to differ, inasmuch as the bilingual may exercise greater control over production and may be able to keep his two languages relatively free of interference in production. Even in perception the two systems may be differentially activated depending on the language expectation established by keeping instructions to a particular language.

It is an empirical fact that bilinguals do indeed perform differently in various psychological/psycholinguistic experiments as compared to monolinguals. The question naturally suggests itself: are these differences associated with specific ways in which the language might be stored in the brain? The neuropsychology of bilingualism is an important field of research.

One way to approach the question is through study of cases of polyglot aphasia. A simplistic analysis would associate a separate area in the brain with each language; if aphasia affects only one of the bilingual's two languages, one could identify the location of the brain lesion and conclude that the affected language was stored at that location. It has been established that the language center of right-handed monolinguals is usually in the left hemisphere and that they suffer from aphasia when that language center has been affected by brain trauma. If a bilingual should experience aphasia in one of his languages after a brain trauma located in the right hemisphere, one might conclude that the affected language was stored in that hemisphere. On the other hand, if the two languages are affected in the same way, one might conclude that the two languages were stored in the same location.

A large number of cases have been described in the literature; Albert and Obler (1978) review 108 case studies. Aphasic deficits that can occur only in polyglot subjects include different types of aphasia in different languages, inability to switch to a second language, inappropriate mixing of the languages, and regression of one language as a second begins to recover. Attempts have been made to explain different recovery patterns. Thus, Ribot's rule states that the first-learned language should be less impaired and should recover first; Pitres's rule states that the most familiar, or most recently used, language returns first in polyglot aphasia. Many examples can be provided for both recovery patterns. When neither rule applies, affective factors may be involved in the order in which languages are recovered. A modification of the affect theory is that the language environment aids a person to recover a certain language. Examples cited include cases of central Asian soldiers with non-Russian first languages who recovered during World War II in a Russian hospital; Russian was the language that returned first.

Gloning and Gloning (1965) studied eleven cases in which precise details of localization of the brain lesion were given, and they added four cases of their own. They tried to correlate the lesion site and the polyglot behavior resulting from the lesion, concluding that no specific brain area is necessarily tied to the phenomenon of polyglot aphasia; rather, they suggest that polyglot aphasia is an overlay to any aphasia and may result from any lesion in the speech region.

Gloning and Gloning also correlated handedness and side of lesion and found that of the four left-handed patients included in their study, three had only a right-hemisphere lesion. Among monolingual left-handed aphasics, 60% have unilateral lesions in the left hemisphere. On this basis, the authors concluded that fluent bilinguals may be less strongly lateralized than monolinguals and that their nondominant hemisphere is involved in their language skills. Albert and Obler (1978) believe that for bilinguals, language is represented in both hemispheres; there is asymmetrical dominance for each language. This ambilaterality consists of relatively weak left lateralization and greater right-hemisphere participation. The right hemisphere appears to play a significant role in the acquisition of a second language. The bilingual is thus distinguished from the monolingual not only in language skills but also in perceptual strategies and patterns of cerebral organization.

After reviewing a large number of clinical and experimental studies that have examined the neurophysiological bases of language processing in bilinguals, Vaid and Genesee (1980) propose a model of hemispheric involvement in second language processing of bilinguals. According to their model, right-hemisphere involvement will be more likely the later the second language is learned relative to the first, the more informal the exposure to the second language, and possibly the earlier the stage of language acquisition. Left-hemisphere involvement is more likely the earlier the second language is learned relative to the first, the more formal the exposure to the second language, and the more advanced the stage of acquisition.

The available evidence suggests that it makes no difference to the child's cognitive development whether he grows up speaking one language or more. Lambert and Tucker (1972) even argue for an intellectual advantage for the bilingual: the bilingual understands that words are only labels (he has at least two labels for most objects), is less likely to confuse the word with the thing, and is therefore more easily capable of abstract thought than the monolingual. In spite of that, there exists widespread prejudice against the bilingual child, who is supposed to be lower in intelligence than the monolingual child.

Saville-Troike (1973) summarized several studies involving Mexican-American, Puerto Rican, and Indian children. Nonverbal intelligence tests given to these children showed no evidence of mental retardation, even though as a group they frequently scored lower than monolingual children on verbal intelligence tests. This may be due partly to the fact that tests are usually conducted in a language the child may not know adequately and partly to social and cultural factors. Personality adjustment problems, reported as being more prevalent among bilinguals than monolinguals, may also be largely due to the bicultural position of the bilinguals. The "marginal man" syndrome described in studies of immigrant culture in America affects individuals who have lost their secure anchoring in their first culture and have not become fully accepted in their second. Inasmuch as language is the primary badge of cultural identity, the epitome of alienation is the person who speaks no language without an accent. The relationship between the bilingual individual and the community in which he finds himself will be discussed in the next chapter.

Recommended Reading

Albert, M. L., and L. K. Obler (1978). *The Bilingual Brain: Neuropsychological and Neurolinguistic Aspects of Bilingualism.* New York: Academic Press.

Grosjean, F. (1982). *Life with Two Languages: An Introduction to Bilingualism.* Cambridge, Mass.: Harvard University Press.

Hornby, P. A., ed. (1977). *Bilingualism: Psychological, Social, and Educational Implications.* New York: Academic Press.

Miracle, A. W., Jr., ed. (1983). *Bilingualism: Social Issues and Policy Implications.* Athens, Ga.: University of Georgia Press.

Paradis, M., ed. (1978). *Aspects of Bilingualism.* Columbia, S.C.: Hornbeam Press.

Chapter 3
Bilingualism: The Bilingual Community

The individual is a member of a community. If this community is monolingual, the individual member is likely to grow up monolingual as well. If the community consists of groups using different languages, the individual has a possibility of acquiring and using more than one language. The ways in which these languages are acquired and used depends on a number of factors, most of which have something to do with the relative prestige of the different groups.

Language is the chief carrier of nonmaterial culture. Thus, it may become the most obvious symbol of the group. Most communities are subdivided into numerous social groupings, such as family, neighborhood, church, occupation, and political affiliation. In multilingual communities language usage often coincides with social groupings. Frequently situations arise in which languages play distinct roles in helping to establish and maintain social groupings. There are many examples in America of churches and schools established by immigrant groups—for example, St. Olaf's College in Minnesota and Suomi College in Michigan, established by Norwegian Lutherans and Finnish Lutherans, respectively, at the time of massive immigration from these countries a few generations ago. The Old Order Amish in Pennsylvania use three languages (or language varieties) in different functions: their home language is German ("Pennsylvania Dutch"), their religious language is High German, and their school language is English.

The Bilingual Community 45

Language has different roles to play within a speech community; even in a monolingual community different speech styles are employed for different roles. A "high style" is used for some functions, such as delivering a sermon in a church, synagogue, or mosque; a "low style" is appropriate in other situations, such as conversing among friends. Being a member of a community requires *communicative competence,* knowing what style is appropriate to use in a given situation (Hymes 1972). Hymes would consider that a theory of language development that included only grammatical competence would imply a child capable of any and all grammatical utterances but not knowing which to use, not knowing even when to talk and when to stop—a cultural monstrosity. By expanding the notion of competence, he emphasizes that the child's knowledge must come to include principles of usage as well as principles of grammar.

There are some societies that are not strictly speaking multilingual but nevertheless use two varieties of the same language under clearly delimited conditions. Ferguson (1959) used the term *diglossia* to refer to such situations, in which a more prestigious, usually relatively more archaic form of a language is used in "High" functions and a relatively less prestigious, colloquial form is used in "Low" functions. Ferguson discussed four situations in detail: Arabic diglossia, Greek diglossia, Swiss German diglossia, and Creole/French diglossia in Haiti. In Arabic diglossia the language of the Koran is used side by side with local vernaculars. In Greece literary Greek (*katharevousa*) serves for High functions, whereas the speech of the people (*dhimotiki*) occupies the Low position. In Switzerland *Schwyzertütsch* is the language of everyday communication for the German-speaking cantons, whereas standard German functions as the High variety. In Haiti these positions are taken by Haitian Creole (a creolized form of pidgin French) and standard French, respectively. In all these cases the speakers regard the High variety as superior to the Low variety in a number of respects. In each case there is a sizable body of highly admired literature, a considerable amount of standardization, and a strong tradition of grammatical study in the High form of the language; this form is usually also grammatically more complex, containing forms and categories that are not present in the Low variety. The High variety is learned largely by formal education and carries with it the prestige conveyed by education. A striking feature of diglossia is the existence of pairs of different lexical designations for common concepts, one used exclusively in the High variety, the other in the Low. The difference between the High and Low varieties of the same language in a diglossia situation is comparable to but not identical with the use of high and low style in a language like English: the formal-informal dimension in English is a continuum, whereas the functional roles of the two varieties in diglossia are sharply delimited and the two forms are largely mutually exclusive.

In a multilingual setting the two varieties of a diglossic speech situation may be represented by two different languages. Language serves as a social symbol: if a social group has relatively high prestige, and that social group is associated with a particular language, the language shares in the prestige of the social group. Social dominance has its counterpart in linguistic dominance. The relative prestige of the languages determines, among other things, the direction of second language acquisition: speakers of the language felt to be socially inferior are likely to learn the language of the group whose language is considered superior, but the converse is much less likely to take place. On the other hand, the pressure experienced by the speakers of the language of lower prestige can lead to the awakening of *language loyalty* in the threatened group; this may produce defensive isolation, practiced for the purpose of maintaining the culture of the group, which is symbolized by its mother tongue.

Schumann (1976) discusses the role of social distance as a factor in second language acquisition. Social distance, and hence a bad language learning situation, will exist when one of the two language groups is dominant, when both groups desire preservation and "high enclosure" for the groups, and when both groups hold negative attitudes toward each other. The term "high enclosure" refers to structural aspects of integration as opposed to cultural aspects. Enclosure involves such factors as institutional separation (separate schools, churches, and so forth), restrictions on marriage outside the group, and tendencies to engage in different professions. The outcome of the contact between the two groups may be assimilation, acculturation, or preservation. If the second language group decides to assimilate, it gives up its own lifestyle and values and adopts those of the target language group. If acculturation is chosen, the second language group adapts to the lifestyle and values of the target language group while maintaining its own cultural patterns for within-group relations. Preservation means that both groups prefer to maintain their own cultural patterns as much as possible. Factors such as cohesiveness and size of the second language group, congruence or lack of congruence between the two cultures, and the second language group's intended length of residence in the target language area also play a role in determining social distance and hence the outcome in terms of linguistic adaptation.

As examples of bad language learning situations, Schumann cites the cases of Americans living in Saudi Arabia and Navajos living in the American Southwest. In the first case one group—the Americans—is considered by both groups at least technically and economically dominant. The two cultures are not congruent, and both sides probably desire high enclosure. Furthermore, the intended stay of the Americans is likely to be relatively short, lasting for the duration of the employment contract, which in most cases amounts to a few years. As a result, social distance between the Americans and the Saudis is considerable, and the American group is unlikely to acquire the language of the local population. In the Navajo case both the Navajos and the English-speaking majority have over a number of years considered the Navajos to be subordinate. Again both sides desire high enclosure; the Navajos also appear to prefer preservation of their own culture rather than assimilation. Considerable social distance prevails, and the learning of the other language is unlikely to take place. These two examples also illustrate the fact that it is usually the member of a subordinate group who learns the language of the dominant group and not vice versa; the conditions do not lead to symmetrical bilingualism.

As an example of a good language learning situation, Schumann cites the case of American Jewish immigrants in Israel. Here the two groups perceive each other as being politically, technically, and culturally equal; the Americans desire assimilation, and this is encouraged by the Israelis; both groups desire low enclosure, cultural differences are minimized, and the immigrants probably intend to stay in the country permanently. Thus, social distance is relatively small, and the newcomers are in a good position to acquire spoken Hebrew.

The attitudes the two language groups hold toward each other are often quite deeply ingrained and may be present in individuals who consider themselves to be totally unprejudiced. There exist research techniques that nevertheless make it possible to explore such hidden attitudes. One of them is the *matched guise* technique, developed by Lambert (1967).

Lambert and coworkers have carried out a series of studies in greater Montreal in Canada, with the dual purpose of evaluating the attitudes of English-speaking and French-speaking Canadians toward each other and assessing the role of language as a badge of identification. The subjects were bilingual speakers of French and English, who produced test materials in both of their languages. The listeners, who were not told that the same speaker appeared in two linguistic guises, were asked to evaluate the personalities of the speakers on several categories relating to competence (intelligence, ambition, self-confidence, leadership, courage), personal integrity (dependability, sincerity, character, conscientiousness, kindness), and social attractiveness (sociability, likeability, entertainingness, sense of humor, affectionateness). The scales also involved such characteristics as religiousness, good looks, and height.

Several different groups of listeners judged the personalities of the matched guise speakers. The ratings given to the same person in the two different guises reveal clearly the social stereotypes prevalent among the population. Thus, a group of listeners consisting of English Canadian males rated speakers in their English Canadian guises as having more character and as being better looking, taller, more intelligent, more dependable, kinder, and more ambitious than the same speakers in their French guises. The male French Canadian listeners apparently shared the same prejudice: they, too, rated the speakers in their English guises as having more character and as being more intelligent, more dependable, and likeable. The French guises were rated higher with respect to kindness and religiousness by their linguistic counterparts. In general, both groups appeared to share the evaluation of French Canadians as being relatively second-rate people.

In another study Lambert used both male and female speakers as matched guises and employed four groups of listeners: English Canadian male, English Canadian female, French Canadian male, and French Canadian female. The results showed some interesting modifications of the earlier results obtained with male speakers and listeners. English Canadian listeners, both men and women, viewed the female speakers more favorably in their French guises. In particular, English Canadian men saw the women as being more intelligent, ambitious, self-confident, dependable, courageous, and sincere in their French than in their English guises. The English Canadian women likewise rated the women as being more intelligent, ambitious, and self-confident (but shorter) in their French than in their English guises. Both English Canadian groups downgraded the male speakers in their French guises. French Canadian male listeners preferred both English Canadian men and women (that is, the speakers in their English guises). French Canadian women listeners, on the other hand, favored male representatives of their own cultural group, even though they, too, preferred English Canadian women. Lambert interprets this outcome as an indication that French Canadian women are guardians of French Canadian culture: anxious to preserve French Canadian values and to pass these on in their own families through language, religion, and tradition, they prefer marriage partners belonging to the same group.

Developmental studies also carried out by Lambert and coworkers revealed that the social attitudes reflected in language preference start around twelve years of age.

Similar studies have been conducted in other language contact situations. For example, Arthur, Farrar, and Bradford (1974) investigated the evaluation of matched guises speaking Chicano English and the local (Los Angeles) standard. The listeners—48 UCLA students in undergraduate linguistics courses—rated four speakers (eight voices) on fifteen semantic differential scales related to success, ability, and social awareness. Dialect differences consistently affected ratings: the Anglo voice was evaluated as belonging to an individual who was more friendly, strong, honest, hardworking, ambitious, upper class, intelligent, dependable, educated, and so on, than the same speaker using the Chicano voice. The authors caution against drawing rash conclusions from the study, noting wryly at the same time that "University students have a reputation for being on the liberal side of most issues, including issues of ethnic and racial tolerance and integration. It appears from this study, however, that the doctrine of equality of dialects voiced by linguists has not fully penetrated the value systems of students in linguistics." The point is, of course, that the technique is capable of tapping unconsciously held attitudes.

Bourhis and Giles (1976) carried the matched guise technique somewhat further. They conducted a matched guise study in a naturalistic setting where listeners had no prior evaluative set, since they were unaware of their participation in an experiment. The test material consisted of a tape-recorded request, addressed to the audience in a theater, to participate in an audience survey by filling in a short questionnaire available in the foyer. The same male bilingual speaker of Welsh and English tape-recorded four versions of the request: in RP (standard British English), in a broad, South Welsh accented English, in a mild, South Welsh accented English, and in a standard, nonlocalized Welsh. Two types of middle-class audiences in Cardiff listened to the various versions of the request. One set of audiences— the Anglo-Welsh set—consisted of Welshmen who were assumed to speak primarily English (according to the authors, only 8% of the 300,000 inhabitants of Cardiff speak Welsh); they were attending two films in English that played at a theater on five consecutive nights. The Anglo-Welsh listeners did not hear the Welsh-language tape. The other set—Bilingual Welsh—were the audiences attending a play staged in Welsh for four consecutive evenings at the same theater. Complying with the request involved considerable effort on the part of the members of the audiences: they had to leave the auditorium, walk through the foyer, ignore the bar, find the questionnaire forms, and finally complete and return them to the box office. At the end of each performance the completed questionnaires were counted and the total audience number was obtained from box office records.

As expected, the response to the different guises was dependent on the interaction between speaker and audience. For the Anglo-Welsh audiences, the standard accent (RP) and the mild South Welsh accent were equally successful in eliciting cooperation; the same plea voiced in the broad Welsh accent was only half as successful. For the Bilingual Welsh audiences, RP was the least successful, the request in Welsh was the most successful, and the two degrees of Welsh accent in English were half as successful as the request made in Welsh. The authors analyze the results in terms of attitudes toward in-group and out-group speech. For bilinguals, the Welsh language is the most salient dimension of Welsh identity. The group who had assembled to watch and hear a play performed in Welsh were most responsive to a request voiced in Welsh and practically ignored the request voiced by a speaker of standard British English. In this case Welsh was obviously the in-group language and English the language of the outgroup. The use of Welsh-accented English may have suggested to that audience that the speaker was a Welshman who was either unable or unwilling to use the Welsh language; the results show clearly that the audience was reluctant to cooperate with the speaker of the out-group language. The study thus illustrates the importance of purpose, setting, and topic—in other words, the social situation—in the listeners' reaction to the perceived ethnicity of a speaker as symbolized by his speech.

A study by Arzapalo (1969) exemplifies the relationship between degree of linguistic assimilation/acculturation and social class. Arzapalo describes the social role of Mayan and Spanish in Yucatan and Guatemala. Social class and language usage are closely correlated. Monolingual Indians occupy the lowest position on the social scale. The lower middle class consists of mestizos and Indians who speak Spanish and are reasonably well acculturated. Their speech shows phonological and syntactic interference from Mayan as well as numerous loanwords, loanshifts, and forms that are attested from literary Spanish of the seventeenth century but are no longer heard in standard Guatemalan Spanish. The middle class, socially superior to the lower middle class, also shows less interference from Mayan in their Spanish. Their speech is characterized, among other things, by hypercorrections (spelling pronunciations). In the speech of the middle class the majority of place names in Yucatan that have glottalized stops in Mayan are pronounced without glottalization. Borrowings from Mayan are largely restricted to designations of indigenous animals, flowers, and food—words that were borrowed into Yucatec Spanish together with the cultural items unknown to European Spaniards. The last stage of the acculturation process is the change of Indian family names to Spanish ones.

Arzapalo suggests that the inhabitants of Yucatan and Guatemala are aware of the correlation between differences in language and racial and socioeconomic patterns. They appear convinced that it is possible and desirable to change their social dialect in order to improve their social standing. Statistics support this statement: the number of Spanish speakers increased from 35% in 1910 to 90% in the 1960s. Arzapalo also observes that it is the mestizos (members of the lower middle class) who have a marked tendency to adopt the speech patterns of the upper classes; the use of the prestige forms of the language serves as a means for upward mobility.

The use of different languages in a multilingual community may also serve to symbolize group solidarity. Denison (1971) describes a situation in which three languages are involved in a complex social structure. The locale of his study was Sauris, a German linguistic island in northeastern Italy, where an archaic form of Southern Bavarian is spoken in addition to the national language, Italian, and the regional language, a dialect of Friulian (a Romance language distinct from Italian, although closely related to it). The German dialect is the language of the family; children acquire Italian at an early age either at home from their parents or in kindergarten; Friulian is the language of communication with the surrounding Friulian-speaking area and serves as a symbol of in-group solidarity among young males who have gone to secondary school in the nearest regional center. The three languages are highly correlated with situational categories. Italian occupies the High end of the scale, German dialect the Low end, and Friulian a position in between. Italian is the language of organized religion and school; it is also used in speaking to outsiders (and to each other when outsiders are present), unless they are known to be speakers of Friulian. Friulian is used with acquaintances from the surrounding Friulian-speaking area and also in their presence with each other. It is also employed habitually by young men when talking to each other and serves as indicator of membership in their group. German dialect is used at home, especially when participants are female adults.

Interference appears to work in the direction from High to Low: Italian and Friulian elements are acceptable when speaking German, and Italian elements when speaking Friulian, but German may not be introduced into Friulian and Italian, and neither German nor Friulian elements are introduced into Italian. Denison observed that segmental intrusions from German into Friulian were extremely rare and were treated with extreme ridicule; interference from Friulian into Italian was encountered slightly more often, and social disapproval was less marked. The oldest speakers showed the least amount of Romance interference in their German; within any age group females showed less interference in their German than males.

Since the functions of the three languages are clearly established and their association with social situations is fixed by tradition, participants in a conversation are to some extent able to create social situations by skillful code switching. Denison describes a situation in which a wife, quarreling with her husband in a bar and trying to persuade him to come home, addressed him in German, while he responded in Friulian. German is the language of the family, and the wife was invoking the claim of family solidarity in trying to get her husband to come home; Friulian is the language of the in-group of young males, the husband's drinking companions, and the husband was emphasizing his solidarity with the company in the bar. In another situation Saurian workmen in Udine, a Friulian-speaking community, were addressed by some locals in Friulian and chose to answer in Italian. The implied demand to be addressed in the prestige language appears to have been motivated by a desire to manipulate the social situation in the direction of greater social equality.

Within a multilingual community language contact can frequently lead to language conflict. It is, of course, the social groups that are in conflict; language is the symbolic issue, the battlefield upon which political and social conflicts can be fought out in disguise.

Inglehart and Woodward (1967) present a well-reasoned argument concerning the relationship between linguistic pluralism and political separatism. They claim that linguistic pluralism does not result in political separatism without certain socioeconomic factors playing a part. The two primary factors are the level of economic and political development attained by the country in question and the degree to which social mobility is blocked because of membership in a given language group. The second factor is related to the first, in that it appears particularly critical in societies undergoing the transitional stages of early industrialization.

At a low level of development the masses are inert and do not participate in the political community. A small elite usually receives education in a cosmopolitan language and assimilates to the majority society. In the transitional stage the masses are "mobilized" but not yet assimilated; it is at this stage of rising expectations that the divisive force exerted by differences in language will be the greatest. At a high level of political-economic development most upwardly mobile individuals have the opportunity to become fluent in one or more foreign languages, mass media transcend linguistic boundaries, the social distance between linguistic groups is minimized, and language conflict is less likely to develop.

In contemporary Western Europe language conflicts are neutralized to a certain degree due to widespread voluntary bilingualism and to the formal equality given the four principal languages (English, French, German, Italian) in supranational European institutions. A survey of six nations carried out in 1962 showed that a majority of adult Dutch and Belgians claimed to understand one or more foreign languages; a quarter of adult Germans and a third of adult French reported that they could understand a foreign language. European institutions use simultaneous translation into the four principal languages; there is no tendency to establish one language as the dominant language.

This has not always been so, and there are still remnants of language conflict in Europe. Belgium is a case in point (Nelde 1983b). Here historical factors have produced a situation in which Flemings constitute the majority of the population, but membership in the Flemish-speaking group carries an implication of lower social status. During the nineteenth century Flemish was practically banished from public life; upward mobility depended upon acquisition of French. Belgium has experienced a number of language riots in the twentieth century, with Flemings demanding equal status for their language in government and military service. It is the strong relationship between membership in a linguistic group and social mobility that lies at the bottom of the language conflict in Belgium.

The United States constitutes a classic case of assimilation, which was greatly influenced by the public school system. The public schools leveled language differences and at the same time created the basis for social mobility. Canada, on the other hand, has developed a classic case of language conflict. The British North-America Act (1867) established unilingualism; one had to know English to advance beyond the menial level. The French-speaking population, concentrated in Quebec, lived under conditions of social and geographical isolation, and in 1967 more than 75% of them were monolingual. By that time, however, French Canada had developed a leadership class, and French Canadians have been increasingly successful in their demands for equal dignity as well as for equal linguistic and political rights. It remains to be seen whether the strong separatist movement in Quebec will finally lead to a political split along linguistic lines.

Another example of language conflict that is related to social mobility can be found in India. There are four major linguistic regions in India, with twelve principal language areas and about 200 languages. The South comprises about 25% of the total population; the languages spoken are Dravidian (Telugu, Tamil, Kannada, Malayalam). The East, with 15% of the population, speaks three Indo-Aryan languages (Bengali, Oriya, Assamese). The West, comprising about 14% of the population, speaks two Indo-Aryan languages (Marathi, Gujarati). The North-Central region, with about 46% of the population, speaks primarily two Indo-Aryan languages (Hindi-Urdu and Panjabi) and one Dardic language (Kashmiri). Hindi is the official language in five states and two union territories. The remaining eleven states recognize each of the eleven major languages for state purposes.

A bilingualism study in 1961 showed that only 9.7% of the population was bilingual. English was claimed by 26% of the total bilingual population; Hindi was next, with 22% of the bilingual population. For intergroup communication purposes, Hindi-Urdu, English, and Sanskrit can be regarded as pan-Indian languages.

After independence was achieved, the question of administrative language had to be resolved. The choice of English, the former colonial language, appears to be closely connected with the question of social mobility. Government jobs have been the chief avenue for upward social mobility in India, and competition for them is sharp. The elite that had administered India under the British colonial regime was generally bilingual in English and a regional language. The less educated masses were excluded from government jobs then and are excluded now, except insofar as the locus of power has shifted to regional centers. Attempts have been made to establish Hindi as the national language, but these attempts have met with strong opposition from speakers of other languages, since this would automatically give the Hindi-speaking group preferential access to political office. The establishment of Hindi as the sole national language is viewed by non-Hindi speakers as Hindi imperialism. English is less divisive, because all groups are more or less equally handicapped.

For a historical example, let us consider the case of the Austro-Hungarian empire. During the eighteenth century the situation was stable; it was based on an agrarian economy and a Latin-speaking elite. Toward the end of the eighteenth century and at the beginning of the nineteenth, increasing urbanization and economic developments brought about the mobilization of new elements, the rise of a middle class, and the awakening of a national consciousness linked to language. When Joseph II tried to establish German as the universal language of the empire in place of Latin, revolts broke out across the land. The Magyars were the first to assert their right to their own language: in 1839 the Diet declared Magyar the official language of government and clergy, and in 1843 Magyar became the exclusive language of the schools. Hungary revolted against Austria in 1848; the revolt was brutally crushed, but after 1866, when Austria had been defeated by Prussia in another war, Magyars achieved equality. The year 1867 marks the birth of the Austro-Hungarian Dual Monarchy, in which each half had its own government, law, and courts.

Ironically, the establishment of Magyar as the state language cut off the principal prerequisite for social mobility from its own minorities. In 1904–1905 Magyars constituted 52% of the population of the Hungarian kingdom, but 91% of the schools were taught in Magyar, and there was not a single Slovak or Ruthenian secondary school.

Croatia was administratively part of Hungary. As long as Latin was the language of administration, there was no problem; but when

Magyar was to replace Latin, a strong opposition developed, which contributed to the rise of group awareness among the Croats and finally played a part in the ultimate dissolution of the empire.

Bohemia was administratively part of Austria. When German was made the official language, the language problem became the main issue of Czech policy. In 1897 Minister Badeni issued decrees requiring all judges in Czech lands to conduct trials in the language of the accused and requiring all civil servants to be bilingual. Since German had been the dominant language and Czech the subordinate one, Czechs were more likely to be bilingual than Germans; the two laws would have established a body of Czech judges and civil servants. Now it was the Germans who rebelled, Badeni was forced to resign, and the decrees were repealed. The language conflict served to sharpen the existing social problems. Combined with other factors, these conflicts contributed to the breakup of the Austro-Hungarian empire after World War I along linguistic lines.

Recommended Reading

Clyne, M. (1972). *Perspectives on Language Contact, Based on a Study of German in Australia*. Melbourne: The Hawthorn Press.

Elias-Olivarez, L., E. A. Leone, R. Cisneros, and J. R. Guttierrez, eds. (1985). *Spanish Language Use and Public Life in the USA*. (Contributions to the Sociology of Language 35.) Berlin and New York: Mouton.

Fasold, R. W. (1984). *The Sociolinguistics of Society*. Oxford: Basil Blackwell.

Gal, S. (1979). *Language Shift: Social Determinants of Linguistic Change in Bilingual Austria*. New York: Academic Press.

Schach, P., ed. (1980). *Languages in Conflict: Linguistic Acculturation on the Great Plains*. Lincoln, Nebr.: University of Nebraska Press.

Veltman, C. (1983). *Language Shift in the United States*. Hawthorne, N.Y.: Mouton de Gruyter.

Chapter 4
Language Contact and Linguistic Convergence

The observation has frequently been made in different parts of the world that some languages spoken in the same geographical area share typological features, even though they may be related only remotely or not at all. Such languages are said to constitute a *Sprachbund*, a language convergence area and the languages spoken within that area, in which genetic heterogeneity is gradually replaced by typological homogeneity. The German term "Sprachbund" was coined by Trubetzkoy; the concept itself was elaborated in an influential article by Jakobson (1931a), in which he described phonological "linguistic alliances" in eastern Asia, northern Europe, and the wide territory comprising eastern Europe and western Asia that he referred to as Eurasia. Later (1938) Jakobson added the important notion of linguistic affinity, claiming that under conditions of language contact, only those elements of structure are accepted by a language from another language that correspond to its own tendencies of development.

Linguistic convergence in a Sprachbund presupposes a situation in which speakers of different languages live in close proximity for centuries and maintain their own language for communication with members of their own group yet also frequently have to communicate with speakers of other languages who reside in the same geographical area. Before discussing some typical cases, let us consider two kinds of situations in which language shift rather than language maintenance is the result.

One way in which languages can come into contact is the arrival of a substantial group of newcomers to a formerly linguistically homogeneous territory. One possible outcome, of course, is that both groups continue to speak their own language; this may ultimately lead to a linguistic alliance—a Sprachbund. The newcomers may be assimilated into the indigenous population and assume their language; or the newcomers' language may prevail, and the original inhabitants may adopt it. Which outcome emerges as a result of the contact situation depends on a large number of extralinguistic factors such as the size of the respective groups, their level of material and nonmaterial culture, and their military strength. Usually a period of widespread bilingualism precedes the language shift.

When the original inhabitants adopt the language of the newcomers, we may assume that during the period of bilingualism they speak the new language with a certain degree of interference from their primary language. If after the shift these elements from the primary language are transmitted to later generations of speakers of the prevailing language, they constitute the *substratum* of that language. Typically, the substratum affects the phonology of the adopted language, but other kinds of interference may likewise be found; in general, the effects of a substratum are comparable to the influence of a bilingual speaker's mother tongue on his secondary language.

When the newcomers are linguistically absorbed into the indigenous population, the influence of their language, the *superstratum,* is comparable to the influence of a bilingual's secondary language upon his primary language. Superstratum influences are usually found in the lexicon, but they may affect other aspects of the language as well.

In the literature the terms "substratum" and "superstratum" are frequently applied to languages occupying the Low and High ends of the prestige scale in multilingual diglossia. This is understandable, since in many cases the newcomers have been military conquerors and therefore have been in a dominant position, whereas the conquered indigenous populations have been in a subordinate position. In the present discussion the terms will be used to refer to language contact situations in which a language shift has taken place, without implications of inferiority or superiority. The choice of the term is simply determined by the direction of the shift. If the indigenous population speaks language A and the newcomers speak language B, and if speakers of A shift to B, then A constitutes the substratum of B. If, on the other hand, speakers of B shift to A, then B constitutes the superstratum for A.

In a Sprachbund situation the languages entering into the linguistic alliance are said to stand in an *adstratum* relationship to each other. Adstratum presupposes language maintenance for a substantial period of time.

A widely studied language convergence area is found on the Balkan peninsula. The languages participating in the Balkan Sprachbund belong to several more or less closely related families. Three Slavic languages are members of the Sprachbund: Bulgarian, Macedonian, and the southeastern dialects of Serbocroatian. The other main languages of the Balkan Sprachbund are likewise Indo-European: Albanian, Modern Greek, and Romanian. Historically, the now extinct Indo-European languages Illyrian and Thracian as well as Latin and Ancient Greek may be assumed to have played a role. Later the non-Indo-European languages of several waves of conquering invaders— Avars, Bulgars, Hungarians, Turks—entered into the picture. The complex history of the Balkans has seen developments in which the language of one set of invaders (for instance, southern Slavs) constitutes the dominant language until the next invasion (in this case by Volga Bulgars, who were speakers of a Turkic language), when it becomes the subordinate language, ultimately emerging victorious when the invaders have been absorbed. Substratum, superstratum, and adstratum influences have to be taken into consideration in attempting to explain the causes of Balkan linguistic convergence.

The structural features shared by the majority of contemporary Balkan languages are called *Balkanisms*. (For a relatively recent summary, see Schaller 1975.) Those shared by the largest number of Balkan languages include the following:

1. *Decay of nominal and pronominal inflection.* All six of the main languages of the Balkan Sprachbund have experienced a reduction of the case system. Usually a construction with a preposition is employed instead. The following examples are from Bulgarian, in which the decay of the nominal inflection has gone farthest. In these examples the preposition *na,* originally with locative meaning, is used to introduce nominal attributes, indirect objects, and direct objects.

Attribute: *knigata na bašta mi* 'my father's book'
Indirect object: *toj kaza na majka* 'he says to the mother'
Direct object: *palento na ogŭn zabraneno* 'lighting fire is forbidden'
Locative: *na koja ulica živeete* 'on which street do you live'

2. *Pleonastic use of personal pronouns.* This feature is likewise found in all six of the main Balkan languages. A Modern Greek example would be *emena me fainetai* 'it seems to me'; compare Macedonian *jas nego go poznavam* 'I know him' (literally, 'I him him know'), Albanian *mua më kunë sjellë këtu* 'they brought me here'.

3. *Loss of the infinitive and its replacement by a personal construction.* This is again one of the common features. Compare Bulgarian *daj mi da pija* 'give me to drink' (literally, 'give me that I drink'), Modern Greek *dos mou na pio* 'give me to drink', Albanian *a-më të pi* 'give me to drink'.

4. *Use of postpositive article.* This feature is shared by five of the six languages (the Modern Greek article precedes its noun). It should be noted that each language has used linguistic material present in the language itself for the development of the postpositive article; we are dealing not with the borrowing of morphemes but with the spread of a pattern. Compare Romanian *elev, elevul* 'pupil, the pupil', *floare, floarea* 'flower, the flower'; Macedonian *učenik, učenikot* 'pupil, the pupil', *zgrada, zgradata* 'building, the building', *utro, utroto* 'morning, the morning'.

A number of additional Balkanisms are shared by different subsets of the six main Balkan languages. For example, the analytic formation of comparatives is shared by the Šopluk dialects of Serbocroatian, Bulgarian, and Modern Greek: 'pretty' and 'prettier' appear as *ubav – po-ubav* in the Šopluk dialects, as *xubav – poxubav* in Bulgarian, and as *kalos – pio kalos* in Modern Greek. The numbers 11 through 19 are formed with the translation equivalents of 'one on ten' in the three Slavic languages, in Romanian, and Albanian: compare *jedanaest* (*jedan + na + deset) in Serbocroatian, *unsprezece* (un + spre + zece) in Romanian, and *njëmbëdhjetë* (një + mbë + dhjetë) in Albanian for 'eleven'.

In addition, the core Balkan languages share many phonological features, such as reduction of unstressed vowels (especially in southeastern Serbocroatian dialects, Macedonian, and Bulgarian); loss of tone and quantity and development of an expiratory accent (particularly noticeable in southeastern Serbocroatian dialects as compared to the standard language and those dialects that are not part of the Sprachbund); development of a central vowel (Bulgarian and Romanian); and development of a special intonation pattern for yes-no questions (Serbocroatian, Romanian, and Albanian; see Lehiste and Ivić 1980). There is also a large collection of shared vocabulary, particularly loanwords from Greek and Turkish, and shared loan translations. The impression of similarity is enhanced by an abundance of habitual sayings, phrases, and idioms that follow the same pattern; for example, 'at a good time' appears in Serbocroatian as *u dobri čas*, in Bulgarian as *dobър čas,* in Greek as *hora kale,* in Romanian as *ceas bun,* and in Albanian as *orë e mbarë.*

Albanian, Bulgarian, Macedonian, and Romanian share the largest number of Balkanisms. Modern Greek and Serbocroatian lack several of the features characteristic of the Balkan Sprachbund; in Serbocroatian frequently only the Torlak and Šopluk dialects appear to be involved in the linguistic alliance.

In trying to establish the causes of the observed linguistic convergence, scholars have attempted to identify one of the languages spoken in the Balkans as the source of the Balkanisms. Substratum and superstratum languages are fairly well known, with the exception of some of the ancient Indo-European languages (Thracian, Illyrian) spoken in the interior of the peninsula while Greek and Latin spread outward from the cities and along the coast. There exists, however, no single language that contains all the features characteristic of the Balkan Sprachbund; attempts to explain them on the basis of a particular substratum or superstratum have been unsuccessful.

The adstratum theory is relatively more plausible. By the fourth century A.D. Latin was spoken extensively in the northern half of the peninsula, and Greek was spoken in the southern half; both languages continued to be spoken and were available as adstratum. The invasions of the ancestors of southern Slavs in the fifth and sixth centuries created the preconditions for the development of linguistic convergence.

The appearance of the various Balkanisms in the Balkan languages can be followed in written records that were continuous in Greek and began at a relatively early date in Bulgarian. Greek provides the earliest examples: the avoidance of the infinitive is already attested in New Testament Greek, and the analytical comparison of adjectives can be found in eighth- and ninth-century manuscripts. This feature is found in Bulgarian in the twelfth century. The merger of the dative and genitive appears in Greek in the tenth century; the use of prepositions to indicate syntactic relationships seems to have begun in Bulgarian in the twelfth century. Greek had always had a definite article; Bulgarian begins to show the development of the article in the eleventh century, and its use becomes regular in the seventeenth century. Because of the lack of written records, Balkanisms cannot be dated any earlier than the sixteenth and seventeenth centuries in Albanian and Romanian. The Balkan Sprachbund appears to have been established by the seventeenth century (Schaller 1975).

Even the adstratum theory cannot fully explain the shared features of the Balkan Sprachbund, and for the same reason that the superstratum and substratum theories were found wanting: there exists no language that contains all the features that characterize the Sprachbund. Civ'jan (1965) has suggested that the Balkanisms can be explained not by reconstructing an earlier stage but by constructing a future stage in the development of the Balkan languages. To represent this future stage toward which the Balkan languages are converging, Civ'jan sets up a syntactic model for sentences in the various languages. The sentence model consists of the same syntactic slots for all languages; the syntactic slots may be filled by lexical items drawn from any one of the languages constituting the Sprachbund. According to this theory, the defining characteristics of the Balkan Sprachbund are similarities in syntax.

As an example of a Sprachbund characterized by phonological—in this case particularly suprasegmental—features, let us reconsider the situation around the Baltic Sea used as an example by Jakobson (1931a) (see Lehiste 1978). Jakobson included the following languages in the Sprachbund: Swedish, Norwegian, most Danish dialects, some north German dialects, North Kashubian, Lithuanian, Latvian, Livonian, and Estonian. In most of these languages Jakobson found distinctive tonal movements on accented syllables or contrastive presence and absence of a glottal modification similar to the Danish *stød*.

Many of the sources available to Jakobson at that time were quite old even for 1930. For example, his information for Lithuanian dated from 1876, for Swedish and Norwegian from 1901, and for North Kashubian from 1903. In my 1978 paper I considered the information that had become available since Jakobson's article appeared, and I arrived at slightly different results.

With respect to the Slavic languages, both Jakobson and Trubetzkoy (1939) based their claims about the presence of tone in northern Kashubian dialects on the *Slovinzische Grammatik* by Lorentz (1903). The dialect has now become extinct; but a reanalysis of Lorentz's data by Stokhof (1973) suggests that the existence of tone at the time described by Lorentz is disputable. Stokhof observed that in Lorentz's conception, pitch was automatically connected with vowel quality differences in stressed vowels. The same vowel quality differences also appeared in unstressed positions. Stokhof concluded that the pitch differences were a concomitant feature of the opposition between tense and lax vowels in stressed position and retranscribed Lorentz's data by indicating vowel quality and position of stress.

Regardless of whether the Slovincian system included distinctive tone or not, the Kashubian dialects do show some differences from their closest Slavic neighbors, namely, the local dialects of Polish. All West Slavic languages went through a stage at which their vowel system was characterized by a long-short opposition, and the prosodic system included free stress. Polish has lost the quantity opposition and has acquired fixed stress on the penultimate syllable. Kashubian has likewise lost the quantity opposition, but its stress system differs from that of Polish. In the Southeast there is bound stress on the first syllable; in Central Kashubian word stress is morphologically motivated but essentially free and mobile. It is difficult to say whether the different treatment of stress is due to internal developments in Kashubian or perhaps to language contact. Free stress is unlikely to have arisen due to contact with German, since German has fixed stress on the stem; the isolation of Kashubian from any contact with Lithuanian (which does have free stress) makes it more likely that the free stress in Central Kashubian is due to language-internal factors and most probably represents an archaic feature. Fixed stress on the first syllable in the Southeast may have some connection with contacts with German, but it should be remembered that other West Slavic languages (Czech, for example) have likewise developed initial stress.

Jakobson's assumption of a complete polytonic circle around the Baltic Sea thus appears not completely valid, as far as the southernmost tip of the territory is concerned. It should be added at this point that the Low German dialects with stød-like characteristics ("rheinische Schärfung") are geographically separated from the Kashubian territory; they may constitute part of a North Sea Sprachbund, but they should not be properly included in the Sprachbund around the Baltic Sea.

The southern and southeastern shores of the Baltic are (or have been previously) the home of Baltic peoples, whose languages preserve the Indo-European polytonicity, albeit in modified form. The German and Polish speakers of that territory have not developed tone; however, there is some evidence that language contact has influenced Polish sentence intonation in the variety of Polish that is in contact with Lithuanian (Nikolaeva 1977).

The prosodic system of Lithuanian appears not to have been essentially modified as a result of its contacts with neighboring languages. The Latvian system, on the other hand, shows considerable influence from Finno-Ugric languages spoken in the same territory and to the north of the area in which Latvian is presently spoken (Zeps 1962). The prosodic system of Latvian differs from that of Lithuanian in two basic respects: in contrast to the free accent of Lithuanian, accent in Latvian is fixed on the first syllable, and Latvian has developed a third tone in addition to the two inherited tones that it shares with Lithuanian. It is generally accepted that these two differences from Lithuanian are due to contact with Livonian, a Finno-Ugric language with stress on the first syllable.

The Latvian third tone, manifested as a glottal modification, is phonetically very similar to the Danish stød (Lehiste 1972). It arose in Latvian in connection with the retraction of word stress to a first syllable that carried an original acute accent (the term is used to refer to the pitch pattern that appears in Lithuanian as a long falling tone and in Latvian as a long even tone). In words that were already accented on the first syllable, the acute continues in Latvian as the long even tone that Endzelin (1923) refers to as *Dehnton*. In words in which the word stress was retracted to an originally unstressed first syllable with the acute, the first syllable now carries the third tone, often referred to as broken tone; the German term is *Stosston*. In classical three-accent areas the sole historical source of the third tone is this reflex of Baltic and Slavic acute. In a number of other dialects, the broken tone goes back both to one of the reflexes of Baltic and Slavic acute and to all reflexes of Baltic and Slavic circumflex; thus, the third tone may also appear in unaccented syllables such as affixes and endings.

Evidence for the claim that the development of the third tone is due to language contact is to be found in a closer study of Latvian dialects (Lekomceva 1974). Latvian is often classified into two main dialects: Low Latvian and High Latvian. Low Latvian, in turn, is divided into the Central dialect and the so-called Tamian or Livonian dialects. Here the term "Livonian" is used to refer to the dialects of Latvian rather than to the Finno-Ugric language of the Livonians. The Tamian dialects are spoken in territories that according to historical and archeological evidence were formerly inhabited by Livonians. In some of the areas Livonian became extinct by the middle of the nineteenth century; it survives in Kurzeme, on the coast, in the speech of a few hundred Latvian-Livonian bilinguals. Now the Tamian dialects exhibit a number of characteristics that are clearly Finno-Ugric in origin. Some of these characteristics have strongly influenced standard Latvian. Among the latter are a great number of Livonian loanwords; Zeps (1962) counted about 80 that are current in the Latvian standard language and stated that approximately 400 Finnic loans are attested in Latvian, even though it is impossible in many cases to decide whether the words came into Latvian from Livonian or from Southern Estonian. Grammatical loans include the development of some characteristic features that are absent in Lithuanian, such as the syntactic model for expressing possession. Old Latvian used the pattern *es turu grāmatu* 'I have book' (Rūķe-Draviņa 1977); contemporary Latvian uses *man ir grāmata* 'to me is book', which is typically Finno-Ugric (the pattern is also found in Russian, where it is also claimed to have arisen due to contact with Finno-Ugric languages; see Veenker 1967).

The Tamian dialects show a large number of additional typically Finno-Ugric features that are likewise found in Livonian. For example, there are some phonemic subsystems in Tamian dialects in which the old Indo-European voiced-voiceless opposition has been reevaluated as tense versus lax, so that voicing has ceased to constitute a distinctive opposition (Zeps 1962). There is even evidence of a breakdown of the grammatical gender system (Endzelin 1923); Livonian, as a Finno-Ugric language, has no grammatical gender. The influence of Livonian upon the development of the Latvian prosodic system thus may be taken as extremely probable, if not certain.

Livonian survives in Kurzeme, albeit precariously, and thus is available for investigation. It can be shown that during the centuries of adstratum relationship, Livonian has, in turn, been influenced by Latvian. The most dramatic parallel between Latvian and Livonian is the presence of tonal oppositions in Livonian. No other Finno-Ugric language has phonemic tone (but see below regarding developments in Estonian and Finnish). Livonian has been variously described as having three tones that are identical with those of Latvian (Posti 1942), as having a phonemic opposition between presence and absence of stød (Zeps 1962), and as having an accentual system involving five types of stressed syllables, of which four are marked each by a specific syllable accent carrying labels like acute, grave, drop, and broken (Viitso 1974). Even if one were to adopt the simplest solution—that Livonian has acquired a phonemic opposition between presence and absence of stød—it still remains necessary to account for the presence of stød in Livonian.

Posti (1942) considers the rise of stød in Livonian to be due to internal factors. Décsy (1965) assumes that stød was borrowed from Latvian relatively late—during the nineteenth century. Interestingly, the presence of stød in Livonian was first recognized by a Dane, Vilhelm Thomsen, in 1890; it is of course no accident that Thomsen himself spoke a language characterized by the presence of stød.

Livonian exhibits many other features, both phonological and grammatical, that can best be explained through extensive borrowing from Latvian. For example, it has borrowed all eleven Latvian verbal prefixes; Livonian, as a Baltic-Finnic language, started out without either verbal prefixes or prepositions (de Sivers 1971).

Taking all factors into consideration, it appears reasonable to assume that the development of tonal oppositions in Livonian is due to language contact and thus can be attributed to the incorporation of Livonian into the Sprachbund around the Baltic Sea.

Jakobson (1931a) included Estonian in the polytonicity Sprachbund on the basis of work by Polivanov (1928). Polivanov's description of Estonian contains many factual mistakes: he cites forms that are morphologically wrong and gives erroneous descriptions of durations and pitch movements. He is nevertheless correct in observing that some durational differences are accompanied by pitch differences. Trubetzkoy (1939) concluded on the basis of Polivanov's description that the pitch differences are phonemic, whereas the quantity differences are automatic concomitants of distinctive tone. As a result, Trubetzkoy reduced the three-way quantity contrast to a two-way contrast, compensating for the loss of one degree of quantity by the introduction of phonemic tone.

The suprasegmental system of Estonian is the subject of much ongoing research and discussion (Lehiste 1980). A survey of the various experimental studies dealing with pitch and duration in Estonian published before 1977 has been compiled by Eek (1977). Among the more interesting results are those of Remmel (1975) and Lippus and Remmel (1976). Remmel found that in overlong quantity the falling fundamental frequency contour may contain a period during which intensity is considerably reduced. This reduction in intensity is especially noticeable when the overlong quantity appears as a diphthong. Remmel identified the intensity drop near the middle of the syllable nucleus with the Danish stød and the Latvian and Livonian broken tone. Remmel has also found a two-peaked tonal contour associated with the illative case. In Estonian many words are in quantity 2 (long) in the genitive and in quantity 3 (overlong) in the partitive and the short illative, the segmental structure remaining constant. Remmel found systematic differences between the tonal contours of overlong vowels in the partitive and the short illative: the falling phase of the tonal contour was longer in the short illative, and it contained a second peak. Lippus and Remmel suggested cautiously that the quantity system of Estonian is in the process of transition and that the development of a distinctive tonal component in Estonian is at least a strong possibility. They did not go so far as to claim the presence of phonemic tone in contemporary Estonian. It should be emphasized here that the tonal features found by Lippus and Remmel are claimed to distinguish between two kinds of overlong words rather than between long and overlong words as had been claimed by Polivanov and Trubetzkoy.

Some support for the argument that Estonian may be in the process of developing tonal distinctions is provided by a study by Lehiste and Danforth (1977). This study offers a statistical interpretation of the results of certain listening tests performed with synthesized Estonian disyllables (Lehiste 1975). Three factors contribute to the identification of suprasegmental patterns on disyllabic words: the duration of the first syllable, the duration of the second syllable, and the pitch contour applied to the whole word. Statistical analysis demonstrates that in a perceptual hierarchy pitch contour ranks higher than the duration of the second syllable.

In my paper on polytonicity (Lehiste 1978) I suggested a tentative explanation for the origin of the pitch patterns that accompany differences between quantities 1 and 2 on the one hand and quantity 3 on the other hand. In many instances overlength in Estonian is the result of the loss of a vowel after a long syllable. Disyllabic sequences without overlength on the first syllable have a step-down pitch contour distributed over the two syllables. It may well be that the loss of the vowel of the second syllable resulted in transferring the tonal contour of the whole disyllabic sequence to the lengthened first syllable, which thus acquired its distinctive falling pattern.

This argument would support spontaneous tonogenesis in Estonian, without any necessary influence from neighboring languages. Nevertheless, some areal factors may be noted that could conceivably argue for linguistic convergence. These include the presence of tone in Lithuanian and Latvian and its spread northward into Livonian (in the direction toward Estonia); the development of the long-overlong opposition, with its associated pitch differences, in Estonian, but not (yet?) in Finnish; and the most recent findings of stød-like phonetic features in overlong syllable nuclei in the illative. Some scholars have claimed that the illative represents a fourth durational category. I consider it more likely that if a new distinction has to arise in words with overlength, that distinction will be based not on duration but on some other parameter that can be independently controlled. The presence of stød in Livonian and its embryonic emergence in Estonian are at least suggestive of linguistic convergence, even if they cannot be taken as conclusive proof (Lehiste 1983).

Another language that participated in the Sprachbund around the Baltic Sea for some time is Baltic German. There is no evidence that Baltic German developed polytonicity, but it appears quite clear that its quantity system differed from that of other German dialects in interesting ways. Hentrich (1925) studied the quantity system of Baltic German experimentally. He measured the duration of plosives following short and long vowels in test words and sentences produced by approximately 25 Baltic German informants. He found that the average duration of the intervocalic plosive in such words as *Nacken* 'neck' was considerably longer than that of the intervocalic plosive in such words as *Haken* 'hook'. In a parallel investigation using speakers of Low German as subjects, Hentrich found that average durations of consonants in the same two types of words were identical. Hentrich's Baltic German subjects were mostly from a territory in which Latvian is spoken by the general populace. Consonant quantity is phonemic in Latvian as well as in Livonian and Estonian. Two conclusions are possible: either that Baltic German introduced the length opposition in consonants on the basis of contacts with Latvian and Estonian, or that the adstratum relationship between these languages contributed toward the preservation of an older quantity system of German that was restructured elsewhere in German-speaking territory. I tend to favor the second conclusion, especially in the light of some data available for Finland-Swedish (Lehiste 1979).

Noting that a more archaic quantity pattern was present in Baltic German than in the Low German territories from which settlers had come to the shores of the Baltic, I became interested in exploring whether a similar situation might not be found in Finland, where Swedish has long been in contact with Finnish. The lack of tone in most dialects of Finland-Swedish is generally attributed to contact with Finnish.

I carried out a small experimental study involving the production and analysis of 26 minimal pairs of the types CVCCV (*kappa* 'cape, cloak') and CVVCV (*kapa* 'to mutilate'), plus 4 words of the type CVCV (*tipi* 'Indian tent') (Lehiste 1979). The words were produced in a constant frame by four speakers of Finland-Swedish in Turku, Finland. Measurements were made of the duration of all segments, and various statistical treatments were applied to the data.

In standard Swedish the stressed syllables of disyllabic words contain either a long vowel, followed by a short consonant, or a short vowel, followed by a long consonant. Finnish has four possible patterns: CVCV, CVVCV, CVCCV, and CVVCCV. Finland-Swedish turned out to have a long-short opposition in both vowels and consonants, which makes it in that respect similar to Finnish. The question now arises whether the Finland-Swedish prosodic system survives from an older system, represents an independent development in Finland-Swedish, or is due to contact with Finnish. Since quantity patterns of the CVCV type (short vowel + short intervocalic consonant) are found in other Swedish dialects, an adstratum relationship with Finnish need not be invoked to explain their existence in Finland-Swedish. The occurrence of long voiceless plosives after long vowels, however, appears not be attested elsewhere in Swedish dialects, and the four speakers who produced the test words in this study realized words like *kapa* (CVVCV) with a long intervocalic plosive. It is possible that the presence of both CVCV and CVVCV word types is entirely due to the survival of the original (early Swedish) quantity system in Finland-Swedish. However, sequences of long vowel + long consonant were not very frequent in the ancestor language, and the pattern appears to have been generalized to instances in which it is not etymologically justified. Influence from a similar Finnish pattern thus appears to be a possible factor contributing to the preservation and extension of the older quantity system.

Although Finnish may have contributed to the disappearance of tone in the majority of Finland-Swedish dialects, there is some recent evidence that certain dialects of Finnish may be in the process of developing contrastive tone (Niemi and Niemi 1981, 1984). In southwestern dialects of Finnish, words of the type CVCV are developing a half-long vowel in the second syllable (the half-long vowel is a well-established feature of words of this type in Estonian). This reduces the phonetic difference between words of the types CVCV and CVCVV (such as *sata* 'hundred' versus *sataa* 'it rains'). One way to maintain a distinction between the two word types is gemination of the intervocalic consonant, and this is indeed observed in many instances. In the southwestern dialects, however, a difference in the fundamental frequency contour is likewise found on the vowels of the second syllable: the fundamental frequency contour starts at a higher value in words of the type CVCV than in words of the type CVCVV. In cases where the durational differences in the second syllable vowel have been neutralized and gemination of the intervocalic consonant does not develop, pitch may indeed acquire distinctive function. It is not claimed that this development is due to language contact; it is nevertheless interesting to note that these dialects of Finnish are spoken in territories adjacent to the Baltic Sea.

The accumulated evidence appears to support the observation that there exists a Sprachbund around the Baltic Sea; but defining it strictly in tonal terms does not do justice to the facts. What seems to emerge is a picture of suprasegmental systems that utilize both quantity and tone. Quantity oppositions are present in all non-Slavic languages around the Baltic Sea, whereas tonal oppositions seem to have receded from Kashubian (if they ever were present) and from Finland-Swedish. On the other hand, new tonal systems have arisen in Latvian and Livonian. The tonal system of Latvian appears to have been restructured and even enriched as a result of contact with Livonian; Livonian has acquired contrastive tone; and Estonian, as well as some Finnish dialects, appears to be developing a tonal component. Polytonicity thus seems to be moving northward along the eastern shores of the Baltic Sea. Its progress is naturally slow: its introduction into

Estonian may be connected with the loss of certain unstressed vowels, which took place in the fourteenth and fifteenth centuries (and resulted in the development of the opposition between long and overlong degrees of quantity). After the passing of five centuries polytonicity is only beginning to acquire a potentially distinctive function in Estonian. But the recent discoveries of potential tonal features in Finnish make it seem not at all impossible that one day the Jakobsonian circle around the Baltic Sea may be closed.

The selection of examples in this chapter (and throughout the book) is determined by my own research interests and my familiarity with the described situation. Many other examples can be found in the literature, and many other language contact situations might have been chosen as illustrations. For example, Sorensen (1972) describes multilingualism in the Northwest Amazon, and Gumperz and Wilson (1977) describe a language contact case from the Indo-Aryan/Dravidian border. The bibliography provides many additional references.

Recommended Reading

Jakobson, R. (1931). "Über die phonologischen Sprachbünde." *Travaux du Circle Linguistique de Prague* 4. Reprinted in *Selected Writings I: Phonological Studies*, 137–143. The Hague: Mouton.

Lehiste, I. (1978). "Polytonicity in the Area surrounding the Baltic Sea." In E. Gårding, G. Bruce, and R. Bannert, eds., *Nordic Prosody: Papers from a Symposium*, 237–247. Travaux de l'Institut de Phonétique de Lund 13.

Sandfeld, K. (1930). *Linguistique balkanique*. Paris: Champion.

Schaller, H. W. (1975). *Die Balkansprachen: Eine Einführung in die Balkanphilologie*. Heidelberg: Carl Winter Universitätsverlag.

Zeps, V. J. (1962). *Latvian and Finnic Linguistic Convergences*. (Indiana University Publications, Uralic and Altaic Series 9.) Bloomington, Ind.: Indiana University Press.

Chapter 5
Results of Language Contact: Pidgins and Creoles

A special kind of language contact situation leads to the development of languages called *pidgins* and *creoles*. We will first consider the characteristics and present status of pidgins and creoles and then explore the conditions under which such languages come into being.

Pidgins and creoles have sometimes been called "mixed" languages. This implies that two or more languages are involved in the creation of a pidgin and/or creole. To be sure, each pidgin or creole is at least lexically related to one or more other languages with which it is not structurally identical. Usually this involves a European language, most frequently English, French, Portuguese, Spanish, or Dutch. A creole that shares most of its vocabulary with another language is traditionally called by the name of that language; for example, a creole that shares most of its vocabulary with English is called an English-based creole or creolized English. The traditional label appears to imply a theory of origin; and the origin of pidgins and creoles is highly controversial. In fact, the study of pidgins and creoles constitutes a vigorous subfield of linguistics, with a long tradition of publication, lively exchange of information, and strongly held views (see, for example, Valdman 1977). In this chapter I can only hope to offer a very condensed summary of a rapidly developing field.

The term "mixed language" also implies that a pidgin or creole has no structure of its own, that it constitutes a blend of two languages (in the case of the creoles of the Caribbean, this would be a mixture of English or French with some African language). This view is no longer considered to be valid, although new examples of mixed languages are presented to linguistic audiences from time to time (see, for example, Rhodes 1977). The current majority opinion considers pidgins and creoles to be genuine languages in their own right, not just corrupted forms of some standard language.

"Pidgin" is a term first used for Chinese Pidgin English and later applied to any language of a similar type. A *pidgin* is a contact vernacular, a spoken language used for communication between speakers who have no other language in common; it is not normally the native language of any of its speakers. The term "pidgin" has been the subject of much research; it is generally assumed that it is an adaptation of the English word *business*. Pidgin English would then be business English. Pidgin English appears to have come into existence as a trading language in Far Eastern seaports. As a first approximation, one might describe a pidgin as a language of limited vocabulary and simple structure, lacking many grammatical categories such as number and gender.

Creole (from the Portuguese word *crioulo,* via Spanish and French) is a term that originally referred to a white man of European descent who had been born and raised in a tropical or semitropical colony. Later the meaning was extended to include indigenous natives and others of non-European origin, such as African slaves. Then the term was applied to certain languages spoken by creoles in and around the Caribbean and West Africa; later it was extended to other languages of similar type. Most creoles, like most pidgins, are European-based; this means that the vocabulary can be identified as having come from one of the European languages. Creole English and Creole French are most common in West Africa and America; Spanish and Portuguese creoles are common in other parts of the world. There are some pidgins and creoles that are not European-based; for example, Chinook Jargon, used for trading by northwestern American Indians, was a pidgin (Silverstein 1972; Thomason 1983). Non-European creoles are also found in Africa.

Unlike a pidgin, a creole is indeed the native language of most of its speakers. Its vocabulary and syntactic devices are sufficient for meeting all the communication needs of its speakers; nevertheless, a creole, like a pidgin, tends to minimize redundancy in its grammar. For example, although pidgin English lacks any plural marker for nouns, creole English has a plural suffix (or clitic): *-dem,* derived from the pronoun *them*. This suffix is normally omitted when plurality can be inferred from other signals. Thus, the standard English forms *the boys, the three boys, those boys* appear in creole English as *di bwai-dem, di trii bwai, dem bwai*. **Di trii bwai-dem,* in which plurality is already indicated by the numeral, does not occur; neither does **dem bwai-dem,* in which plurality is already marked in the pronoun corresponding to *those.*

A creole is inferior to its corresponding standard language only in social status; linguistically speaking, it is a full-fledged language. A pidgin, however, is so limited both lexically and structurally that it is suitable only for specialized and limited communication.

If interlingual contact is maintained for a long time, language shift may take place: one group may learn the language of the other. If the two groups are of approximately equal size and status, a stable bilingualism may result. A pidgin usually arises when the groups are not of equal status; and under certain conditions a pidgin may evolve into a creole. This happens when a creole acquires a sufficient number of native speakers: children who learn a pidgin as their first language. In the transition from pidgin to creole, syntax and vocabulary are extended; the language may become stabilized, and a creole may become the native language of a community. Bloomfield (1933) appears to have been the first to suggest this historical relationship between pidgins and creoles. Hall (1966) carried the idea much further, postulating something like a linguistic life cycle.

Various creoles are spoken at the present time by more than six million people in and around the Caribbean and by smaller and more scattered groups in West Africa, southern Asia, and Southeast Asia. There are more than four million speakers of French creoles in the Caribbean; four major dialects, mutually intelligible, are found in Haiti, the former French Guiana, in Louisiana, and on the Lesser Antilles. Creole French is also spoken on the island of Reunion and the British island of Mauritius, both in the Indian Ocean.

Creole English is spoken by about two million people in Jamaica and on other Caribbean islands and in West Africa. Sranan and Saramaccan, two mutually unintelligible dialects of creole English, are still spoken by about 80,000 people in Surinam, even though that territory passed from British into Dutch hands in 1667. Gullah, a dialect of creole English, was once widely spoken in Georgia and South Carolina and on the nearby Sea Islands; it is now extinct on the mainland and becoming rare on the islands.

Spanish and Portuguese creoles are widely spoken in the Far East and on the West African coast. Papiamentu is a creole spoken in the southern Caribbean in which Spanish and Portuguese elements are intermingled, so that the classification is disputed; DeCamp and Hancock (1974) call it a sort of creolized Esperanto. Other European-based creoles are found in South Africa and in Hawaii. An interesting case is Pitcairnese, which is the creole descendant of the pidgin English used by the original *Bounty* mutineers who reached the island in 1790.

Historical evidence is available about some pidgins that are no longer in use, such as Russenorsk, the trade language used by Russian and Norwegian mariners in the barter trade carried on in the White Sea (Broch and Jahr 1984). Many other "mixed languages" that are not usually thought of as creoles have many creole characteristics, such as Yiddish, Indonesian, and Swahili.

Origins of Pidgins and Creoles

There exist two main theories concerning the origins of pidgins and creoles. The *monogenetic theory,* which we will consider first, postulates a single common origin for all pidgins and creoles; the *polygenetic theory* allows for spontaneous generation of new pidgins under conditions favorable for their creation.

Navarro-Tomas (1951) argued that Papiamentu was not an indigenous Caribbean blend of Portuguese and/or Spanish with African elements, claiming that it instead originated in the Portuguese pidgin used as a trade jargon in West Africa during the slave trade. Whinnom (1956) demonstrated that four Spanish creoles of the Philippines were not independent developments but had all diverged from a common source in the Moluccas, and that underlying these Spanish creoles was a Portuguese pidgin very similar to that of Goa in India. Whinnom's book drew attention to the great importance of Portuguese pidgin, which during the sixteenth century replaced Arabic and Malay as the trade language of the Far East. This pidgin was used by traders of all nationalities from India to Indonesia and as far north as Japan.

Whinnom suggested that the Asian Spanish creoles were not simply restructured Spanish but rather a Portuguese pidgin "relexified" under later Spanish influence. The term *relexification* refers to a very rapid replacement of the vocabulary of a language by lexical items taken from another language. Arguments were later presented that the Chinese elements in pidgin English were only secondary and that pidgin English was also a relexification of pidgin Portuguese. If this is true, the case for monogenesis of the Far Eastern pidgins and creoles indeed appears strong.

Taylor (1956, 1957, 1960, 1961) emphasized the similarities among the Caribbean creoles and their many parallels with the creoles of the Far East, suggesting that both Papiamentu and Sranan were relexifications of pidgin Portuguese. Thompson (1961) argued for a parallel development of all the pidgins and creoles—Caribbean, African, and Far Eastern—from Portuguese sources. Stewart (1962) discussed the functions of structure and lexicon in linguistic relationships and concluded that the divergent relexification of a single proto-pidgin was a more tenable hypothesis than the convergent restructuring of the grammars of a whole group of separate languages.

Whinnom (1965) identified the putative proto-pidgin as Sabir, the famous lingua franca of the Mediterranean. Sabir, according to Whinnom, is the source of all European-based pidgins and creoles of the world. Sabir is at least as old as the Crusades; texts survive from the early sixteenth century. The language became moribund after the French conquest of North Africa but was still alive when it was described by Schuchardt in 1909. It appears quite possible that a predominantly Portuguese version of Sabir (or a Portuguese relexification of it) was indeed the pidgin that in the sixteenth century was carried to the Far East as well as to West Africa, where its creole descendant is still spoken on Cape Verde and other islands. From West Africa this pidgin was carried to America, where it formed the basis not only of Papiamentu but also of English, French, and Dutch creoles. It is certainly a fact that a Portuguese origin can be established for many words shared by pidgins in places as remote from each other as Africa, the South Pacific, and China. Examples include the verb *savvy* 'to know' and the noun *pickaninny* 'native child' from Portuguese *saber* 'to know' and *pequeno, pequenino* 'small', respectively (Cassidy 1971).

The supporters of monogenesis would thus speak of an Anglicized creole rather than creolized English. There is very little documentary evidence for the postulated spread of subsequent relexifications of an original proto-pidgin. The argument is basically reduced to Stewart's question: Which is more likely, replacement of the lexicon or convergent structural development? The supporters of the monogenetic theory find it more plausible that the similarities between the creoles are due to descent from a common source; they argue that the influences that can bring about the wholesale adoption of, say, French vocabulary in French colonial territories are clear and obvious, whereas there is no known influence that would explain why the structures of five different European languages should have been modified in precisely the same fashion.

The weaknesses of the monogenetic theory include the sketchiness of the historical documentation, the controversial status of Far Eastern pidgin English, which lacks many of the features shared by other pidgins and creoles, and the problem of residue. There is no question that some pidgins and creoles exist that must have developed without any Portuguese influence, such as Chinook (Silverstein 1972; Thomason 1977), Pitcairnese (Ross and Moverley 1964), and several forms of Amerindian pidgin English (Hancock 1971).

The *polygenetic theory* assumes that pidgins appear by spontaneous generation whenever and wherever the need for them arises (Hall 1966). Normally this occurs during a relatively casual, short-term contact between groups that do not have a language in common. A pidgin can arise—even in the space of a few hours—whenever an emergency situation calls for communication on a minimal level of comprehension. The pidgin will draw its vocabulary from the two or more languages involved in the contact situation; the phonology and syntax will be dramatically simplified, so that the pidgin is suitable only for minimal and specialized communication. Most pidgins disappear as quickly as they arise.

If the interlingual contact is prolonged and institutionalized (for example, in connection with slavery or long-time occupation of a country by foreign troops), the pidgin becomes fixed, and newcomers to that interlingual scene must learn it. The pidgin may then be expanded to make it suitable for a greater variety of speech situations, either externally by borrowing additional features from the basic languages involved or internally by analogical improvisations on the resources of the original pidgin. So begins the process of evolution that may lead to the creation of a creole, if a generation of children grows up for whom the pidgin constitutes the native language. According to Hall, all creoles have evolved from pidgins and may evolve further into "normal" languages, thus completing their "life cycle."

Pidgins and creoles may be extended to new communities by a process of diffusion. This appears to have been the case with pidgin English in Melanesia. Creole French became institutionalized and was introduced to the colonies along with the expansion of colonial French rule.

The question still remains concerning the causes of similarities between creoles whose sets of original interlingual components apparently had nothing in common. These similarities are too great for coincidence. They include elimination of inflections for number in nouns and for gender and case in pronouns, identity of adverb and adjective, use of iteration for intensification, development of compound prepositions using the Portuguese particles *na* and *de*, use of verbal aspects marked by syntactic particles rather than true tenses, and so on. If we were to explain these similarities as a result of diffusion, we would be moving rapidly toward the monogenetic theory.

Defenders of the monogenetic theory argue that one way in which a pidgin may arise is through stimulus diffusion. It is a fact that certain creoles such as Pitcairnese share many common creole characteristics, even though no direct Portuguese influence can be shown to have been present in their evolution. This may be explained as being due neither to direct descent nor to totally independent creation, but to stimulus diffusion. If a person with even a casual familiarity with any form of pidgin participates in the spontaneous creation of a new pidgin, the resulting language will not be a random mixture of two languages but will inevitably be influenced by the pattern of the pidgin already known. The European settlers on Pitcairn Island were seamen—the mutineers of the *Bounty*—and it is extremely unlikely that none of them had had any experience with some pidgin-like trade language spoken in the harbors of the world.

A more recent explanation of the similarities of pidgins and creoles relates these similarities to linguistic universals (Bickerton 1974, 1975, 1981). The pidgins and creoles are claimed to share those features that constitute universal characteristics of languages. Neither direct descent from a common proto-pidgin nor stimulus diffusion is necessary: given a situation in which a new language of communication is needed, general linguistic principles come into play; given a situation in which a child learns a pidgin as his first language, innate linguistic principles take over, and a language is born that shares in the universal properties of human language.

Thomason and Kaufman (1977) place creolization within a larger framework of language contact. According to the authors, contact-induced language change can result in either language shift or language maintenance. The least amount of interference arises in the case of perfect shift. Moderate to heavy interference is involved in situations in which the language whose speakers have shifted to another language leaves traces in the successor language described earlier as influences of substratum and/or superstratum.

The most extreme interference occurs in *abrupt creolization,* which constitutes a case of language shift in which only the vocabulary of the second language is successfully acquired. In cases of language maintenance, light to heavy interference is found in borrowing, and heaviest normal interference in the situation referred to as a Sprachbund. Most extreme interference in the case of language maintenance takes place when only vocabulary is maintained; this situation, the opposite of abrupt creolization, is called *jargonization.*

In the case of abrupt creolization the shift is so unsuccessful that the shifting speakers acquire only the target-language vocabulary, but not the target-language phonology, morphology, or syntax. Thomason and Kaufman claim that the Caribbean creoles are not creolized pidgins—that in fact there was no pidgin state at all, due to the "pathological nature of their base-line linguistic setting," namely, the massive importation of slave labor and the mixing of slaves with different linguistic backgrounds.

Jargonization occurs when the entire grammar of language A is lost, the vocabulary alone being retained. This is likely to occur in situations of unilateral multilingualism: language B may become so universally known to speakers of A that they can shift to B should they so desire. Most or all of the vocabulary of A may be preserved as a special vocabulary that is available for use when one wants to conceal the content of the conversation. There are jargonized languages like Gypsy Spanish or Anglo-Romany. "If the ethnic group which has shifted to B, but maintained the vocabulary of A as a jargon, maintains its own ethnic identity and should separate itself from the remaining speakers of B (either socially or geographically), users of jargonized A may replace the vocabulary of B entirely by that of A, thereby producing a nativized or creolized jargon" (Thomason and Kaufman 1977). B is then spoken with the vocabulary of A, but with the phonology, morphology, and grammar of B; an example might be the language of English Gypsy children. In a creolized jargon the grammatical structure and the phonology are still those of B, but the vocabulary is that of the original language.

Although creolized jargons share the historical feature of nongenetic development with abrupt creoles and nativized pidgins—all three types show different sources for lexicon and grammar—the jargons differ from the two more traditional types in having a single source for their grammar. Abrupt creoles and pidgins, by definition, do not derive their grammatical system intact from any single language; creolized jargons do, also by definition, and this fact makes them easier to detect in retrospect.

Sociolinguistics and Pidgin-Creole Studies

Creolists agree that sociolinguistic factors were important to the origin of pidgins, though they may disagree on their degree of importance. The supporters of the polygenetic position adopt a primarily sociolinguistic explanation for the origin of a pidgin, emphasizing the frequency of spontaneous generation of new pidgins. Supporters of the monogenetic position hold that the sociolinguistic situation usually only initiates the same two processes that are common to all language history: diffusion and divergence of an already existing pidgin.

Most creolists agree, however, that sociolinguistic factors are very important in the subsequent history of pidgins and creoles. Once a pidgin has been created or imported into a community, its continued survival and its evolution toward creole status and beyond both depend entirely on its role in the society, not on its inherent structure.

The drastically limited vocabulary and syntactic devices of a pidgin do not in themselves lessen the chance of its survival, though they may condition adverse social prejudices that can constitute a threat to its continued existence. If the interlingual situation that first brought a pidgin into a community remains unchanged, the pidgin will normally also remain, and with very little change. If not, then its subsequent development depends mainly on two factors: its social status relative to the standard language of the community, and the variability of the language and the culture. A pidgin invariably, and a creole almost invariably, has low social status. If the equivalent European language is also the standard language of the community, the creole is especially unlikely to be granted status as a real language; rather, it is thought of as a barbarous corruption of the standard language. A typical situation is found in Jamaica, where the creole is inseparably associated with poverty and ignorance, and where those ambitious for social mobility strive diligently to acquire the middle-class standard. There exists a linguistic continuum between the so-called broader varieties of creole and standard English, which is correlated with a continuum of social standing. Similar situations exist in other creole areas, particularly in areas where English constitutes the lexical base.

A counterreaction can be observed as a result of recent political and social developments. One variety of pidgin English, Neo-Melanesian, was given official status under German rule; now it constitutes the national language of Papua New Guinea and seems to be on its way toward creolization. In West Africa a group of Negroes were repatriated from Jamaica to Sierra Leone in the nineteenth century, and their descendants speak a creolized form of their language called Krio. By the middle of the twentieth century Krio came to be one of the symbols of nationalist feeling among those in the region who are violently opposed to the continuation of British influence and wish to make Krio as different from English as possible, even in its orthography. This process could be called *hypercreolization*.

Pidgins and creoles are capable of sudden and massive changes if the social factors are present that bring such changes about; for example, relexification of a creole can take place within a generation, if a colonial territory changes hands and the rulers introduce a new language of administration. Some creoles show a great degree of variation; others are relatively stable. Creole French is essentially mutually intelligible wherever it is found; normally it is not mutually intelligible with standard French, and in areas that have been under French rule we can observe the development of diglossia, with French serving as the High variety and creole as the Low variety. English creoles, however, are extremely variable. Even the two principal dialects of English-based creole in Surinam, Sranan and Saramaccan, are both mutually unintelligible and unintelligible to speakers of other English creoles.

The situation in Jamaica illustrates the development of what is called a *postcreole community*. There is a great deal of geographical dialect variation, especially in vocabulary, and there exists a socioeconomically oriented continuum of speech varieties ranging from "broad creole" or "broken language" to standard Jamaican English (which most speakers assume to be identical with standard British English), with a large number of intermediate varieties. The two extremes are mutually unintelligible, but each Jamaican speaker commands a span of this continuum and is capable of making adjustments up or down, depending on the interlocutor and the audience.

A speech community can reach postcreole status under two conditions. First, it is necessary that the dominant official language be the same as the creole vocabulary base. If it is different, either the creole persists with very little change (as have the English creoles of Surinam, where the official language since 1667 has been Dutch), or it becomes extinct. Second, the social system must provide for sufficient social mobility and sufficient corrective pressures from above (for example, from schools and other institutions), so that the standard language can exert a real influence on the creole speakers and *decreolization*—a process in which a creole becomes gradually more similar to the standard language of its lexical base—can begin. In other words, the standard language must be available. This seems to be the case in Jamaica, which is a typical case of a postcreole community. It is assumed that Hawaii, the Gullah areas, and the other islands of the formerly British West Indies are likewise postcreole areas. A considerable literature has grown up concerning the possible creole origins—and currently ongoing decreolization—of North American Black English. (For a recent treatment of the topic, see Rickford 1986.)

If there exists a rigid caste system that minimizes the availability of the standard language as a model for speakers of a creole, the creole and the standard remain sharply separated, as has been the case in the French areas.

The problem of postcreole variability requires further study. Political and social implications need to be taken into account. For example, the command of the creole can be an asset to a politician. The political success of at least one Jamaican leader is attributed to his conscious and successful efforts to learn the speech and the social mores of the people of his slum constituency; despite his white middle-class background, he is reported to be able to talk with the people, not at them. (It is likewise rumored that before entering politics, he had been a publishing scholar in anthropology.)

Pidginization and Second Language Learning

The polygenetic theory of the origins of pidgins can at the present moment be tested in several industrialized European countries that have, in the years following World War II, acquired large numbers of foreign workers. Several projects have been undertaken to study the linguistic adaptation of those "guest workers" to the linguistic situation in which they find themselves. A typical case is the linguistic acculturation of "guest workers" in Germany (Clyne 1984).

Schumann (1978) has developed a theory according to which second language acquisition under the conditions experienced by the "guest workers" exemplifies the process of pidginization. Schumann recalls Bühler's division of the functions of language into the communicative, the integrative, and the expressive. The integrative function of language is to establish the status of its speakers as members of a group. The expressive function is to display one's linguistic skills. The communicative function is to transmit denotative referential information. Pidginization occurs, according to Schumann, when a language is restricted to its communicative function and is not used for integrative and expressive functions.

The restriction of a language to its communicative functions results from the learner's social and/or psychological distance from the target-language group. According to Schumann, factors that determine the social distance between the group learning a second language and the target-language group include the following:

1. Whether the target-language group, relative to the second-language-learning group, is politically, technically, culturally, or economically dominant, nondominant, or subordinate
2. Whether the integration pattern of the second-language-learning group is assimilation, acculturation, or preservation
3. The second-language-learning group's degree of enclosure
4. The cohesiveness of that group
5. The size of the group
6. Whether the cultures of the two groups are congruent
7. The attitudes of the two groups toward each other
8. The second-language-learning group's intended length of residence in the target-language area

Schumann (1978) discusses in detail each factor and its contribution to the creation of a favorable or unfavorable situation for the acquisition of the target language.

Factors that determine the psychological distance include language shock, culture shock, and culture stress. Language shock involves the learner's inability to name objects and ideas correctly, which results in a fear of being ridiculous and in a sense of shame. Culture shock results from disorientation encountered upon entering a new culture. A healthy person entering a new culture has a repertoire of problem-solving mechanisms; in the new cultural setting it frequently happens that they do not produce anticipated results. New problems mean new demands on one's supply of energy. Though the extreme symptoms of culture shock may pass relatively quickly, more subtle problems may persist and produce culture stress that can last for months or years. Culture stress often centers around questions of identity. For example, the alien may have a university degree and yet be treated as a member of the lower working class. The general who becomes a taxi driver or the lawyer who works as a janitor suffers from cultural stress long after he may have overcome the first language shock.

Schumann takes the position that social and psychological distance are the primary factors hindering second language development. His pidginization hypothesis predicts that where social and psychological distance prevails, pidginization will persist in the speech of second language learners. To substantiate his claim, he offers the results of a research project undertaken in 1973, involving a ten-month longitudinal study of the untutored acquisition of English by six native speakers of Spanish. Data collection involved the recording of both spontaneous and experimentally elicited speech. Schumann presents detailed data for one of the six subjects, a 33-year-old Costa Rican who evidenced very little linguistic development during the course of the project. This man spoke a reduced and simplified form of English in which inflectional morphemes tended to be absent and auxiliary development was minimal; his English had many characteristics of a typical pidgin. Three causes were considered for his lack of development: lack of ability, social and psychological distance, and age. Schumann presents a well-reasoned argument that the subject's persistence in his reduced and simplified English usage was primarily due to his social and possibly also his psychological distance from English speakers.

Recommended Reading

Hall, R. (1966). *Pidgin and Creole Languages*. Ithaca, N.Y.: Cornell University Press.

Hymes, D., ed. (1971). *Pidginization and Creolization of Languages*. London: Cambridge University Press.

Schumann, J. H. (1978). *The Pidginization Process: A Model for Second Language Acquisition*. Rowley, Mass.: Newbury House.

Valdman, A., ed. (1977). *Pidgin and Creole Linguistics*. Bloomington, Ind.: Indiana University Press.

Glossary

adstratum
Language entering into a linguistic alliance in a Sprachbund situation.
Balkanism
Structural feature shared by the majority of contemporary Balkan languages.
bilingual
A person who is able to produce grammatical sentences in more than one language.
calque
See loan translation.
code switching
Switching from one language to another in the course of a conversation.
communicative competence
Knowledge of the appropriate style or language to use in a given situation.
contrastive analysis
Comparison of the structures of language A and language B, for the purpose of predicting errors made by learners of language B and designing teaching materials that will take account of the anticipated errors.
compound bilingual
A bilingual who has acquired his two languages in the same settings and uses them interchangeably in the same settings
coordinate bilingual
A bilingual who has learned his two languages in separate settings.

Glossary

creole
A language claimed to have descended from a pidgin, having become the native language (first language) of the children of a group of pidgin speakers.

diglossia
A situation in which a more prestigious form of a language is used in "High" functions and a relatively less prestigious, colloquial form is used in "Low" functions.

foreign accent
Carryover of the pronunciation of sounds in language A into the pronunciation of sounds in language B.

grammatical interference
Use of features from the grammar of language A in the production of language B.

hypercorrection
Overapplication of a rule in an inappropriate fashion due to mistaken belief in its correctness; overgeneralization of a rule.

interference
Deviations from the norms of either language that occur in the speech of bilinguals as a result of their familiarity with more than one language.

lexical interference
Changes in the lexicon of language B due to contact with the lexicon of language A.

loanshift
A change in the meaning of a morpheme in language A on the model of language B.

loan translation
A type of lexical interference consisting of translation of morphemes of language A into language B.

overdifferentiation
Imposition of phonemic distinctions from the primary language system on the sounds of the secondary system.

phonic interference
Perception and reproduction of the sounds of a bilingual's secondary language in terms of his primary language.

phonotactic interference
Carryover of distributional restrictions of language A into language B.

Glossary

pidgin
A contact vernacular, a spoken language used for communication between speakers who have no other language in common.

reinterpretation of distinctions
The process of distinguishing phonemes of the secondary system by features that are distinctive in the bilingual's primary system but merely concomitant or redundant in the secondary system.

relexification
Very rapid replacement of the vocabulary of a language by lexical items taken from another language.

sound substitution
Replacement of a sound in language B by a sound in language A.

Sprachbund
A language convergence area and the languages spoken within that area, in which genetic heterogeneity is gradually replaced by typological homogeneity.

substratum
Primary language of a group of speakers who have shifted from speaking their primary language to speaking another, adopted language.

superstratum
Former language of a group of speakers who have been linguistically absorbed into a population that continues to speak its primary language.

syntactic interference
Carryover of syntactic patterns from language A into language B, or interpretation of patterns of language B in terms of patterns of language A.

transfer of rules
Application of a rule characteristic of language A in the production of utterances in language B.

underdifferentiation
Failure to distinguish two sounds in the secondary system because their phonetic counterparts are not distinguished in the primary system.

Bibliography

Alatis, J. E., ed. (1970). *Bilingualism and Language Contact: Anthropological, Linguistic, Psychological, and Sociological Aspects.* Washington, D.C.: Georgetown University Round Table on Languages and Linguistics.

Alatis, J. E., ed. (1978). *International Dimensions of Bilingual Education.* Washington, D.C.: Georgetown University Round Table on Languages and Linguistics.

Albert, M. L., and L. K. Obler (1978). *The Bilingual Brain: Neuropsychological and Neurolinguistic Aspects of Bilingualism.* New York: Academic Press.

Albin, A., and R. Alexander (1972). *The Speech of Yugoslav Immigrants in San Pedro, California.* The Hague: Martinus Nijhoff.

Ardener, E., ed. (1971). *Social Anthropology and Language.* London: Tavistock Publications.

Arthur, B., D. Farrar, and G. Bradford (1974). "Evaluation Reactions of College Students to Dialect Differences in the English of Mexican-Americans," *Language and Speech* 17:255–270.

Arzapalo, R. (1969). "The Social Role of the Indigenous Languages of Mexico and Guatemala." *Canadian Journal of Linguistics* 14:133–141.

Bakos, F. (1977). "Les éléments roumains du lexique hongrois et quelques problèmes de l'emprunt linguistique." *Acta Linguistica Academiae Scientiarum Hungaricae* 27:111–159.

Becker-Dombrowski, C. (1981). "Zur Situation der deutschen Sprache im Elsass." In Ureland (1981), 149–180.

Bellmann, G. (1976). "Slawisch-deutsche Mehrsprachigkeit und Sprachwandel." *Sprache der Gegenwart* 41:249–259.

Beltramo, A., and A. de Porcel (1975). "Some Lexical Characteristics of San Jose Spanish." In Hernandez-Chavez, Cohen, and Beltramo (1975), 122–137.

Bickerton, D. (1974). "Creolization, Linguistic Universals, Natural Semantax and the Brain." *Working Papers in Linguistics* (University of Hawaii) 6.3:124–141.

Bickerton, D. (1975). *Dynamics of a Creole System*. New York: Cambridge University Press.

Bickerton, D. (1981). *Roots of Language*. Ann Arbor, Mich.: Karoma.

Biondi, L., S. J. (1975). *The Italian-American Child: His Sociolinguistic Acculturation*. Washington, D.C.: Georgetown University Press.

Bloomfield, L. (1933). *Language*. New York: Holt, Rinehart & Winston.

Blount, B. G., and M. Sanchez, eds. (1977). *Sociocultural Dimensions of Language Change*. New York: Academic Press.

Bourhis, R. Y., and H. Giles (1976). "The Language of Cooperation in Wales: A Field Study." *Language Sciences* 42:13–16.

Breinburg, P. (1981). "Creolese and Sranan: Two New Ethnolinguistic Minorities in Western Europe, with Special Reference to Lexical Items." In Ureland (1981), 265–284.

Broch, I., and E. H. Jahr (1984). "Russenorsk: A New Look at the Russo-Norwegian Pidgin in Northern Norway." In Ureland and Clarkson (1984), 21–65.

Caramazza, A., G. Yeni-Komshian, E. Zurif, and E. Carbone (1973). "The Acquisition of a New Phonological Contrast: The Case of Stop Consonants in French-English Bilinguals." *Journal of the Acoustical Society of America* 54: 421–428.

Cassidy, F. G. (1971). "Tracing the Pidgin Element in Jamaican Creole." In Hymes (1971), 203–221.

Champagnol, R. (1973). "Organisation sémantique et linguistique dans le rappel libre bilingue." *Année Psychologique* 73:115–134.

Civ'jan, T. V. (1965). *Imja ̀suščestvitel'noe v balkanskix jazykax*. Moscow: Nauka.

Civ'jan, T. V. (1977). "O postroenii sintaksisa v grammatike balkanskogo jazykovogo sojuza." *Balkanskij lingvističeskij sbornik*. Moscow: Nauka.

Clyne, M. (1972). *Perspectives on Language Contact, Based on a Study of German in Australia*. Melbourne: The Hawthorn Press.

Clyne, M. (1975). *Forschungsbericht Sprachkontakt*. Kronberg / Ts.: Scriptor-Verlag.

Clyne, M. (1984). *Language and Society in the German-Speaking Countries*. Cambridge: Cambridge University Press.

Cowan, W., ed. (1977). *Actes du huitième congrés des Algonquinistes*. Ottawa: Carleton University.

Craffonara, L. (1981). "Die kulturelle und politische Situation der Selladiner (Frühjahr 1981)." In Ureland (1981), 81–110.

Dalrymple-Alford, E. (1968). "Interlingual Interference in a Color-naming Task." *Psychonomic Science* 10:215–216.

Dalrymple-Alford, E., and A. Aamiry (1969). "Language and Category Clustering in Bilingual Free Recall." *Journal of Language Learning and Language Behavior* 8:762–768.

Das Gupta, J. (1970). *Language Conflict and National Development*. Berkeley and Los Angeles: University of California Press.

Das Gupta, J. (1970). *Language Politics and Language Planning in Modern India*. Berkeley and Los Angeles: University of California Press.

DeCamp, D., and I. F. Hancock, eds. (1974). *Pidgins and Creoles: Current Trends and Prospects*. Washington, D.C.: Georgetown University Press.

Décsy, G. (1965). *Einführung in die finnisch-ugrische Sprachwissenschaft*. Wiesbaden: Harrassowitz.

Decurtins, A. (1981). "Zum deutschen Sprachgut im Bündnerromanischen: Sprachkontakt in diachronischer Sicht." In Ureland (1981), 111–138.

Denison, N. (1968). "Sauris: A Trilingual Community in Diatypic Perspective." *Man* 3.4:578–592.

Denison, N. (1971). "Some Observations on Language Variety and Plurilingualism." In Ardener (1971), 157–183.

Diebold, R. A. (1964). "Incipient Bilingualism." In Hymes (1964), 495–508.

Diekmann, E. (1981). "Zur Situation des Okzitanischen als sprachliche und kulturelle Minderheit in Frankreich." In Ureland (1981), 181–200.

Dorian, N. D. (1981). *Language Death: The Life Cycle of a Scottish Gaelic Dialect*. Philadelphia: University of Pennsylvania Press.

Dressler, W., and R. Wodak-Leodolter (1977). "Language Death." *International Journal of the Sociology of Language* 12:33–44.

Eek, A. (1977). "Experiments on the Perception of Some Word Series in Estonian." *Estonian Papers in Phonetics* (1977), 7–33.

Eichler, E., ed. (1984). *Sprachkontakt im Wortschatz dargestellt an Eigennamen*. Wissenschaftliche Beiträge der Karl-Marx-Universität Leipzig (Leipzig).

Elias-Olivarez, L., E. A. Leone, R. Cisneros, and J. R. Guttierrez, eds. (1985). *Spanish Language Use and Public Life in the USA*. (Contributions to the Sociology of Language 35.) Berlin and New York: Mouton.

Eliasson, S. (1974). "Contrastive Analysis of Phonological Rules." *Reports from Uppsala University Department of Linguistics* 3:28–34.

Eliasson, S. (1981), "Review article: From languages in contrast to interlanguage", *Nordic Journal of Linguistics* 4,2: 161–173

Elman, J. L., R. L. Diehl, and S. E. Buchwald (1977). "Perceptual Switching in Bilinguals." *Journal of the Acoustical Society of America* 62:971–974.

Emeneau, M. B. (1956). "India as a Linguistic Area." *Language* 32.1:3–16.

Endzelin, J. (1923). *Lettische Grammatik*. Heidelberg: Carl Winter Univertätsverlag.

Ervin, S. M., and C. E. Osgood (1954). "Second Language Learning and Bilingualism." *Journal of Abnormal and Social Psychology* 49 (4, pt. 2):139–146.

Espinosa, A. M., Jr. (1957). "Problemas lexicograficos del español del sudoeste." *Hispania* 40.1:139–143. Reprinted in Hernandez-Chavez, Cohen, and Beltramo (1975).

Evers, K. W. (1970). "The Effects of Bilingualism on the Recall of Words Presented Aurally." Doctoral dissertation, University of Minnesota (Dissertation Abstracts 1970:5197A).

Fasold, R. W. (1973). *Tense Marking in Black English*. Washington, D.C.: Center for Applied Linguistics.

Fasold, R. W. (1984). *The Sociolinguistics of Society.* Oxford: Basil Blackwell.

Ferguson, C. A. (1959). "Diglossia." *Word* 15:324–340. Reprinted in Giglioli (1972), 232–251.

Filipović, R., ed. (1975). *Contrastive Analysis of English and Serbo-Croatian.* Vol. 1. Zagreb: Institute of Linguistics, University of Zagreb.

Filipović, R. (1977). "English Words in European Mouths and Minds." *Folia Linguistica* 11:195–206.

Filipović, R., ed. (1982). *The English Element in European Languages.* Vol. 22 *Reports and Studies.* Zagreb: Institute of Linguistics, University of Zagreb.

Fishman, J. A. (1965a). "Bilingualism, Intelligence, and Language Learning." *Modern Language Journal* 49:227–237.

Fishman, J. A. (1965b). "Varieties of Ethnicity and Language Consciousness." *Georgetown University Monograph Series on Language and Linguistics* 18:69–79.

Fishman, J. A. (1966). *Language Loyalty in the U.S.* The Hague: Mouton.

Fishman, J. A. (1967). "Bilingualism with and without Diglossia; Diglossia with and without Bilingualism." *Journal of Social Issues* 23.2:29–38.

Fishman, J. A. (1968a). "Sociolinguistic Perspective on the Study of Bilingualism." *Linguistics* 39:21–50.

Fishman, J. A., ed. (1968b). *Readings in the Sociology of Language.* The Hague: Mouton.

Fishman, J. A., and R. L. Cooper (1971). "The Interrelationships and Utility of Alternative Bilingualism Measures." In Whiteley (1971b), 126–144.

Francescato, G. (1981). "Friulian." In Ureland (1981), 139–148.

Frank, H. (1981). "Demokratische Zweisprachigkeit in Europa: Möglichkeiten einer europäischen Sprachpolitik unter Berücksichtigung der sprachlichen Minderheiten." In Ureland (1981), 17–40.

Fries, C., and K. L. Pike (1949). "Coexistent Phonemic Systems." *Language* 25:29–50.

Gal, S. (1979). *Language Shift: Social Determinants of Linguistic Change in Bilingual Austria.* New York: Academic Press.

Games, S. (1978). "Some Effects of Bilingualism on Perception." In Weinstock (1978), 352–359.

Gerasimova, N. G., ed. (1976). *Grammatičeskij stroj balkanskix jazykov: Issledovanija po semantike grammatičeskix form.* Leningrad: Nauka.

Giglioli, P. P., ed. (1972). *Language and Social Context.* (Modern Sociology Readings.) Harmondsworth: Penguin.

Gloning, I., and K. Gloning (1965). "Aphasien bei Polyglotten." *Wiener Zeitschrift für Nervenheilkunde* 22:362–397.

Goggin, J., and D. Wickens (1971). "Proactive Interference and Language Change in Short-term Memory." *Journal of Verbal Learning and Verbal Behavior* 10:453–458.

Grosjean, F. (1982). *Life with Two Languages: An Introduction to Bilingualism.* Cambridge, Mass.: Harvard University Press.

Gumperz, J. (1982). *Discourse Strategies.* (Studies in Interactional Sociolinguistics 1.) Cambridge: Cambridge University Press.

Gumperz, J. J., and E. Hernandez (1971). "Cognitive Aspects of Bilingual Communication." In Whiteley (1971b), 111–125.

Gumperz, J., and R. Wilson (1971). "Convergence and Creolization: A Case from the Indo-Aryan/Dravidian Border." In Hymes (1971), 151–168.

Haarmann, H. (1975). *Soziologie und Politik der Sprachen Europas.* Munich: DTV Wissenschaftliche Reihe 4161.

Haarmann, H. (1978). *Balkanlinguistik (1): Areallinguistik und Lexikostatistik des balkanlateinischen Wortschatzes.* Tübingen: TBL Verlag Gunter Narr.

Hagström, B. (1984). "Language Contact in the Faroes." In Ureland and Clarkson (1984), 171–189.

Hall, R. (1966). *Pidgin and Creole Languages.* (Ithaca, N.Y.: Cornell University Press.

Hancock, I. F. (1971). "A Survey of the Pidgins and Creoles of the World." In Hymes (1971), 509–523.

Harrison, W., C. Prator, and G. R. Tucker (1975). *English-Language Policy Survey of Jordan: A Case Study in Language Planning.* Washington, D.C.: Center for Applied Linguistics.

Haugen, E. (1950). "Problems of Bilingualism." *Lingua* 2.1:271–290.

Haugen, E. (1956). *Bilingualism in the Americas: A Bibliography and Research Guide.* American Dialect Society. University of Alabama.

Haugen, E. (1956–57). "Problems of Bilingual Description." *Language Learning* 7.3–4:17–23.

Haugen, E. (1969). *The Norwegian Language in America: A Study in Bilingual Behavior.* Bloomington, Ind.: Indiana University Press.

Haugen, E. (1973). "The Curse of Babel." In Haugen and Bloomfield (1973), 33–43.

Haugen, E., and M. Bloomfield, eds. (1973). *Language as a Human Problem.* New York: Norton.

Heath, J. G. (1984). "Language Contact and Language Change." *Annual Review of Anthropology* 13:367–384.

Hentrich, K. (1925). "Experimentalphonetische Studien zum baltischen Deutsch." *Abhandlungen des Herder-Instituts zu Riga,* Erster Band, Nr. 3.

Heras, I., and K. Nelson (1972). "Retention of Semantic, Syntactic, and Language Information by Young Bilingual Children." *Psychonomic Science* 29:391–393.

Herman, S. R. (1961). "Explorations in the Social Psychology of Language Choice." *Human Relations* 14:149–164. Reprinted in Fishman (1968b), 492–511.

Hernandez-Chavez, E., A. D. Cohen, and A. F. Beltramo, eds. (1975). *El Lenguaje de los Chicanos: Regional and Social Characteristics Used by Mexican-Americans.* Arlington, Va.: Center for Applied Linguistics.

Hesseling, D. C. (1979). *On the Origin and Formation of Creoles.* Edited and translated by T. L. Markey and P. T. Roberge. Ann Arbor, Mich.: Karoma.

Highfield, A., and A. Valdman, eds. (1981). *Historicity and Variation in Creole Studies.* Ann Arbor, Mich.: Karoma.

Hill, K. C., ed. (1979). *The Genesis of Language: The First Michigan Colloquium.* Ann Arbor, Mich.: Karoma.

Hintzman, D., R. Block, and N. Innskeep (1972). "Memory for Mode of Input." *Journal of Verbal Learning and Verbal Behavior* 11:741–749.

Hornby, P. A., ed. (1977). *Bilingualism: Psychological, Social, and Educational Implications*. New York: Academic Press.

Hymes, D., ed. (1964). *Language in Culture and Society*. New York: Harper & Row.

Hymes, D., ed. (1971). *Pidginization and Creolization of Languages*. London: Cambridge University Press.

Hymes, D. (1972). "On Communicative Competence." In Pride and Holmes (1972), 269–293.

Ianco-Worrall, A. D. (1972). "Bilingualism and Cognitive Development." *Child Development* 43:1390–1400.

Inglehart, R. F., and M. Woodward (1967). "Language Conflicts and Political Community." *Comparative Studies in Society and History* 10:27–45. Reprinted in Giglioli (1972), 358–377.

Jakobson, R. (1931a). "Über die phonologischen Sprachbünde." *Travaux du Cercle Linguistique de Prague* 4. Reprinted in Jakobson (1962), 137–143.

Jakobson, R. (1931b). "K xarakteristike evrazijskogo jazykovogo sojuza." Reprinted in Jakobson (1962), 144–201.

Jakobson, R. (1938). "Sur la théorie des affinités phonologiques entre les langues." Reprinted in Jakobson (1962), 234–246.

Jakobson, R. (1962). *Selected Writings I: Phonological Studies*. The Hague: Mouton.

Kachru, B. B. (1982). *The Other Tongue: English across Cultures*. Urbana, Ill.: University of Illinois Press.

Kachru, B. B. (1983). *The Indianization of English: The English Language in India*. Delhi: Oxford University Press.

Karttunen, F. (1985). *Nahuatl and Maya in Contact with Spanish*. Austin, Tex.: University of Texas Press.

Kattenbusch, D. (1981). "Die provenzalische Minderheit in Süditalien." In Ureland (1981), 41–52.

Keim, I. (1978). *Gastarbeiterdeutsch: Untersuchungen zum sprachlichen Verhalten türkischer Gastarbeiter. Pilotstudie*. Tübingen: TBL Verlag Gunter Narr.

Kintsch, W. (1970). "Recognition Memory in Bilingual Subjects." *Journal of Verbal Learning and Verbal Behavior* 9:405–409.

Kintsch, W., and E. Kintsch (1969). "Interlingual Interference and Memory Processes." *Journal of Verbal Learning and Verbal Behavior* 8:16–19.

Kloss, H. (1981). "Unorthodoxe Betrachtungen über Volksgruppen und Volksgruppensprachen in Europa." In Ureland (1981), 1–16.

Kolb, H., and H. Lauffer, eds. (1977). *Sprachliche Interferenz.* Halle, Saale: Niemeyer.

Kolers, P. A. (1963). "Interlingual Word Association." *Journal of Verbal Learning and Verbal Behavior* 2:291–300.

Kolers, P. A. (1964). "Specificity of a Cognitive Operation." *Journal of Verbal Learning and Verbal Behavior* 3:244–248.

Kolers, P. A. (1965). "Bilingualism and Bicodalism." *Language and Speech* 8:122–126.

Kolers, P. A. (1966a). "Interlingual Facilitation of Short-term Memory." *Journal of Verbal Learning and Verbal Behavior* 5:314–319.

Kolers, P. A. (1966b). "Reading and Talking Bilingually." *American Journal of Psychology* 79:357–376.

Kolers, P. A. (1968). "Bilingualism and Information Processing." *Scientific American,* March 1968, 78–86.

Krakowian, B., and S. Pit Corder (1978). "Polish Foreigner Talk." *Work in Progress* 11:78–86. Department of Linguistics, Edinburgh University.

Krashen, S. D. (1981). *Second Language Acquisition and Second Language Learning.* Oxford: Pergamon Press.

Kremnitz, G., ed. (1979). *Sprachen im Konflikt.* (Tübinger Beiträge zur Linguistik 117.) Tübingen: TBL Verlag Gunter Narr.

Labov, W., P. Cohen, C. Robins, and J. Levis (1968). *A Study of Non-Standard English and Puerto Rican Speakers in New York City.* Vol. 1: *Phonological and Grammatical Analysis.* Cooperative Research Project No. 3288, U.S. Office of Education.

Lambert, W. E. (1967). "A Social Psychology of Bilingualism." *Journal of Social Issues* 23:91–108. Reprinted in Pride and Holmes (1972), 336–349.

Lambert, W. E., and S. Fillenbaum (1959). "Pilot Study of Aphasia among Bilinguals." *Canadian Journal of Psychology* 13:28–34.

Lambert, W. E., J. Havelka, and C. Crosby (1958). "The Influence of Language Acquisition Contexts on Bilingualism." *Journal of Abnormal and Social Psychology* 56:239–244.

Lambert, W. E., M. Ignatow, and M. Krauthamer (1968). "Bilingual Organization in Free Recall." *Journal of Verbal Learning and Verbal Behavior* 7:207–214.

Lambert, W. E., R. C. Gardner, R. Olton, and K. Tunstall (1968). "A Study of the Roles of Attitudes and Motivation in Second-Language Learning." In Fishman (1968b), 473–491.

Lambert, W. E., and G. R. Tucker (1972). *Bilingual Education of Children: The St. Lambert Experiment.* Rowley, Mass.: Newbury House.

Lamothe, P. L. (1974). "Semantic Generalization in French and English Bilinguals." *Canadian Journal of Behavioral Science* 4:414–419.

Lance, D. M. (1969). *A Brief Study of Spanish-English Bilingualism: Final Report.* Research Project ORR-Liberal Arts-15504, Texas A & M University, August 25.

Lance, D. M. (1975). "Spanish-English Code Switching." In Hernandez-Chavez, Cohen, and Beltramo (1975), 122–137.

Langendoen, D. T. (1970). *Essentials of English Grammar.* New York: Holt, Rinehart & Winston.

Lehiste, I. (1965). "A Poem in Halbdeutsch and Some Questions concerning Substratum." *Word* 21:55–69.

Lehiste, I. (1971). "Grammatical Variability and the Difference between Native and Non-native Speakers." In Nickel (1971), 69–74.

Lehiste, I. (1972). "Some Observations concerning the Third Tone in Latvian." In Valdman (1972), 309–315.

Lehiste, I. (1975). "Experiments with Synthetic Speech concerning Quantity in Estonian." In *Congressus Tertius Internationalis Fenno-Ugristarum*, Tallinn 1970, 254–269. Tallinn: Valgus.

Lehiste, I. (1978). "Polytonicity in the Area surrounding the Baltic Sea." In E. Gårding, G. Bruce, and R. Bannert, eds., *Nordic Prosody: Papers from a Symposium*, 237–247. Travaux de l'Institut de Phonétique de Lund 13.

Lehiste, I. (1979). "A Note concerning Quantity in Finland-Swedish." *Sanomia*, Publications of the Department of Finnish and General Linguistics of the University of Turku 9:129–135.

Lehiste, I. (1980). "Estonian Linguistics: State of the Art." *General Linguistics* 20.4:194–208.

Lehiste, I. (1983). "Prosodic Change in Progress: Evidence from Estonian." In Rauch and Carr (1983), 10–27.

Lehiste, I., and D. G. Danforth (1977). "Foneettisten vihjeiden hierarkia viron kvantiteetin havaitsemisessa." *Virittäjä* 4/1977:404–411.

Lehiste, I., and P. Ivić (1980). "The Intonation of Yes-or-No Questions—A New Balkanism?" *Balkanistica* 6:45–53.

Lekomceva, M. I. (1974). "K tipologičeskoj xarakteristike fonologičeskix sistem dialektov latyšskogo jazyka." *Balto-Slavjanskie issledovanija*, Akademia Nauk SSSR, 227–241. Moscow: Nauka.

Lemarchand-Unger, B. (1981). "Die Verwendung der bretonischen Sprache unter soziolinguistischen Aspekten." In Ureland (1981), 201–218.

Leopold, W. F. (1939–49). *Speech Development of a Bilingual Child*. 4 vols. Evanston, Ill.: Northwestern University Press.

Leopold, W. F. (1948). "The Study of Child Language and Infant Bilingualism." *Word* 4:1–17.

Le Page, R., ed. (1961). *Proceedings of the Conference on Creole Language Studies* (1959). (Creole Language Studies 2.) London: Macmillan.

Lerea, L., and R. LaPorta (1971). "Vocabulary and Pronunciation Acquisition among Bilinguals and Monolinguals." *Language and Speech* 14:293–300.

Lewis, E. G. (1965). *The Bilingual Child: Report on an International Seminar on Bilingualism in Education*. London: Her Majesty's Stationery Office.

Liepman, D., and J. Saegert (1974). "Language Tagging in Bilingual Free Recall." *Journal of Experimental Psychology* 103:1137–1141.

Lippus, U., and M. Remmel (1976). "Some Contributions to the Study of Estonian Word Intonation." *Estonian Papers in Phonetics* 1976:37–65. Tallinn.

Lopez, M., R. Hicks, and R. Young (1974). "Retroactive Inhibition in a

Bilingual A-B, A-B' Paradigm." *Journal of Experimental Psychology* 103:85–90.

Lopez, M., and R. Young (1974). "The Linguistic Interdependence of Bilinguals." *Journal of Experimental Psychology* 102:981–983.

Lorentz, F. (1903). *Slovinzische Grammatik*. St. Petersburg: Akademie der Wissenschaften.

McCormack, P. D. (1977). "Bilingual Linguistic Memory: The Independence-Interdependence Issue Revisited." In Hornby (1977), 57–66.

McCormack, P. D., and S. P. Colletta (1975). "Recognition Memory for Items from Unilingual and Bilingual Lists." *Bulletin of the Psychonomic Society* 6:149–151.

Mack, M. (1982). "Voicing-dependent Vowel Duration in English and French Monolingual and Bilingual Production." *Journal of the Acoustical Society of America* 71:173–178.

Mackey, W. F. (1962). "The Description of Bilingualism." *Canadian Journal of Linguistics* 7:51–85. Reprinted in Fishman (1968b), 554–584.

Mackey, W. F. (1965). "Bilingual Interference: Its Analysis and Measurement." *The Journal of Communication* 15.4:239–249.

Macnamara, J. (1967). "The Linguistic Independence of Bilinguals." *Journal of Verbal Learning and Verbal Behavior* 6:729–736.

Meid, W., and K. Heller, eds. (1981). *Sprachkontakt als Ursache von Veränderungen der Sprach- und Bewusstseinsstruktur*. Innsbruck: Institut für Sprachwissenschaft der Universität Innsbruck.

Miracle, A. W., Jr., ed. (1983). *Bilingualism: Social Issues and Policy Implications*. Athens, Ga.: University of Georgia Press.

Mohan, P., and P. Zador (1986). "Discontinuity in a Life Cycle." *Language* 62:291–319.

Mollay, K. (1976). "Deutsch-ungarische Sprachkontakte." *Sprache der Gegenwart* 41:280–284.

Molony, C., H. Zobl, and W. Stolting, eds. (1977). *Deutsch im Kontakt mit anderen Sprachen/German in Contact with Other Languages*. Kronberg/Ts.: Scriptor-Verlag.

Muysken, P. (1983). "Review Article: *Roots of Language*, by Derek Bickerton." *Language* 59:884–892.

Navarro-Tomas, T. (1951). "Observaciones sobre el papiamento." *Nueva revista de filologia hispanica* 7:183–189.

Nelde, P. H. (1981). "Zur Problematik von Sprachzählungen." In Ureland (1981), 219–224.

Nelde, P. H. ed. (1983a). *Gegenwärtige Tendenzen der Kontaktlinguistik.* Bonn: Ferd. Dummlers Verlag.

Nelde, P. H. (1983b). "Language Contact and Language Shift in Brussels." *Folia Linguistica Historica* 4.1:101–117.

Nickel, G., ed. (1971). *Papers in Contrastive Linguistics.* Cambridge: Cambridge University Press.

Nickel, G. (1983). "Contrastive Linguistics, Error Analysis, and Their Relevance for Language Planning including Language Minimization." In Nelde (1983b), 341–353.

Nida, E. A., and W. L. Wonderly (1971). "Communication Roles of Languages in Multilingual Societies." In Whiteley (1971b), 57–74.

Niemi, J., and S. Niemi (1981). "Finnish Half-Long Vowels, Gemination and Word-Tone." In I. Savijärvi, ed., *Occasional Papers* 1. (Publications of the Department of Languages, University of Joensuu, 6.) Joensuu.

Niemi, J., and S. Niemi (1984). "Word Tone and Related Matters in the Finnish Southwest." In C.-C. Elert, I. Johansson, and E. Strangert, eds., *Nordic Prosody III.* (Acta Universitatis Umensis 59.) Stockholm: Almqvist & Wiksell.

Nikolaeva, T. M. (1977). *Frazovaja intonacija slavjanskix jazykov.* Moscow: Nauka.

Paradis, M., ed. (1978). *Aspects of Bilingualism.* Columbia, S.C.: Hornbeam Press.

Persoons, Y. (1981). "Neubelgien Malmedy." In Ureland (1981), 251–264.

Pike, K. L. (1960). "Toward a Theory of Change and Bilingualism." *Studies in Linguistics* 15:1–7.

Polivanov, E. D. (1928). *Vvedenie v jazykoznanie dlja vostokovednyx vuzov.* Leningrad.

Polkki, M. (1977). "Finnish, English, or Both? A Descriptive Survey of the Choice of Language among Thunder Bay Finns." *Papers from the Transatlantic Finnish Conference,* Texas Linguistic Forum 5:119–128.

Poplack, S., and D. Sankoff (1984). "Borrowing: The Synchrony of Integration." *Linguistics* 22:99–135.

Posti, L. (1942). *Grundzüge der livischen Lautgeschichte.* (Mémoires de la Société Finno-Ougrienne 85.) Helsinki.

Pride, J. B., and J. Holmes, eds. (1972). *Sociolinguistics.* Harmondsworth: Penguin.

Prohovnik, B. (1978). "Linguistic Aspects of Bilingual Aphasia." *Lund University Working Papers* 16:137–152.

Quix, M.-P. (1981). "Altbelgien Nord." In Ureland (1981), 225–236.

Rauch, I., and G. F. Carr, eds. (1983). *Language Change.* Bloomington, Ind.: Indiana University Press.

Remmel, M. (1975). "The Phonetic Scope of Estonian: Some Specifications." *Preprint KKI-5.* Academy of Sciences of the Estonian SSR, Institute of Language and Literature. Tallinn.

Rhodes, R. (1977). "French Cree: A Case of Borrowing." In Cowan (1977), 6–25.

Rice, F. A., ed. (1962). *Study of the Role of Second Languages in Asia, Africa, and Latin America.* Washington, D.C.: Center for Applied Linguistics.

Rickford, J. R. (1986). "Social Contact and Linguistic Diffusion: Hiberno-English and New World Black English." *Language* 62:245–289.

Riegel, K. F., and I. W. M. Zivian (1972). "A Study of Inter- and Intralingual Associations in English and German." *Language Learning* 22:51–63.

Rischel, J. (1983). "Language Policy and Language Survival in the North-Atlantic Parts of Denmark." In Nelde (1983b), 203–212.

Ritchie, W. C., ed. (1978). *Second Language Acquisition Research: Issues and Implications.* New York: Academic Press.

Rohr, R. (1981). "Sprachliche Minderheiten in Europa am Beispiel des Kalabro-Albanischen." In Ureland (1981), 53–58.

Roider, U. (1981). "Zweisprachigkeit und grammatische Inter- und Transferenz im Keltischen der Britannischen Inseln." In Ureland (1981), 285–296.

Rose, R. G. (1975). "Introspective Evaluations of Bilingual Memory Processes." *Journal of General Psychology* 93:149–150.

Rose, R. G., and J. F. Carroll (1974). "Free Recall of a Mixed Language List." *Bulletin of the Psychonomic Society* 3:267–268.

Rose, R. G., P. R. Rose, N. King, and A. Perez (1975). "Bilingual Memory for Related and Unrelated Sentences." *Journal of Experimental Psychology/ Human Learning and Memory* 1:599–606.

Ross, A. S. C., and A. W. Moverley (1964). *The Pitcairnese Language*. London: Deutsch.

Rubin, J. (1962). "Bilingualism in Paraguay." *Anthropological Linguistics* 4.1:52–58.

Rubin, J. (1968). "Bilingual Usage in Paraguay." In Fishman (1968b), 512–530.

Rūķe-Draviņa, V. (1971). "Word Associations in Monolingual and Multilingual Individuals." *Linguistics* 74:66–84.

Rūķe-Draviņa, V. (1977). *The Standardization Process in Latvian: Sixteenth Century to the Present*. (Acta Universitatis Stockholmiensis, Stockholm Slavic Studies 11.) Stockholm: Almqvist & Wiksell.

Sachs, J. S. (1967). "Recognition Memory for Syntactic and Semantic Aspects of Connected Discourse." *Perception and Psychophysics* 2:437–442.

Saegert, J., E. Hamayan, and H. Ahmar (1975). "Memory for Language of Input in Polyglots." *Journal of Experimental Psychology/Human Learning and Memory* 1:607–613.

Saegert, J., S. Kazarian, and R. K. Young (1973). "Part-Whole Transfer with Bilinguals." *American Journal of Psychology* 86:537–546.

Saegert, J., J. Obermeyer, and S. Kazarian (1973). "Organizational Factors in Free Recall of Bilingually Mixed Lists." *Journal of Experimental Psychology* 97:397–399.

Samarin, W. J. (1968). "Lingua Francas of the World." In Fishman (1968b), 660–672.

Sandfeld, K. (1930). *Linguistique balkanique*. Paris: Champion.

Sankoff, D. (1978). *Linguistic Variation: Models and Methods*. New York: Academic Press.

Sankoff, G. (1972). "Language Use in Multilingual Societies: Some Alternate Approaches." In Pride and Holmes (1972), 33–51.

Saville, M. R., and R. C. Troike (1971). *A Handbook of Bilingual Education*. Arlington, Va.: Center for Applied Linguistics.

Saville-Troike, M. R. (1973). *Papers in Applied Linguistics*. (Bilingual Education Series 2.) Washington, D.C.: Center for Applied Linguistics.

Schach, P., ed. (1980). *Languages in Conflict: Linguistic Acculturation on the Great Plains*. Lincoln, Nebr.: University of Nebraska Press.

Schaller, H. W. (1975). *Die Balkansprachen: Eine Einführung in die Balkanphilologie*. Heidelberg: Carl Winter Universitätsverlag.

Schouten, M. E. H. (1977). "Imitation of Synthetic Vowels by Bilinguals." *Journal of Phonetics* 5:273–283.

Schubert, G. (1982). *Ungarische Einflüsse in der Terminologie des öffentlichen Lebens der Nachbarsprachen*. Berlin: in Kommission bei Otto Harrassowitz, Wiesbaden.

Schuchardt, H. (1909). "Die Lingua franca." *Zeitschrift für romanische Philologie* 33:441–461.

Schumann, J. H. (1976). "Social Distance as a Factor in Second Language Acquisition." *Language Learning* 26:135–143.

Schumann, J. H. (1978). *The Pidginization Process: A Model for Second Language Acquisition*. Rowley, Mass.: Newbury House.

Schumann, J. H. (1982). "Simplification, Transfer, and Relexification as Aspects of Pidginization and Early Second Language Acquisition." *Language Learning* 32.2:337–366.

Scollon, R., and S. B. K. Scollon (1979). *Linguistic Convergence: An Ethnography of Speaking at Fort Chipewyan, Alberta*. New York: Academic Press.

Segalowitz, N., and W. E. Lambert (1969). "Semantic Generalization in Bilinguals." *Journal of Verbal Learning and Verbal Behavior* 8:559–566.

Silva-Corvalan, C. (1986). "Bilingualism and Language Change: The Extension of *Estar* in Los Angeles Spanish." *Language* 62:587–608.

Silverstein, M. (1972). "Chinook Jargon: Language Contact and the Problem of Multilevel Generative Systems." *Language* 48:378–406, 596–625.

Simoes, A., Jr., ed. (1976). *The Bilingual Child: Research and Analysis of Existing Educational Themes*. New York: Academic Press.

de Sivers, F. (1971). *Die lettischen Prefixe des livischen Verbs.* Nancy: Imprimerie Berger-Levrault.

Skala, E. (1976). "Der deutsch-tschechische Bilinguismus." *Sprache der Gegenwart* 41:260–279.

Skutnabb-Kangas, T. (1978). "Semilingualism, Cultural Assimilation, and Structural Incorporation: The Case of Finnish Immigrant Children in Sweden." In Weinstock (1978), 514–523.

Sojat, A. (1981). "Resultate des Kontakts der kroatischen Standardsprache mit der urbanen Umgangssprache Zagrebs." In Ureland (1981), 59–68.

Sondergaard, B. (1981). "The Fight for Survival: Danish as a Living Minority Language South of the Danish-German Border." In Ureland (1981), 297–306.

Sorensen, A. P., Jr. (1972). "Multilingualism in the Northwest Amazon." In Pride and Holmes (1972), 78–93.

Sprache und Kommunikation ausländischer Arbeiter (1975). Heidelberger Forschungsprojekt "Pidgin-Deutsch." Kronberg/Ts.: Scriptor-Verlag.

Stewart, W. A. (1962). "Creole Languages in the Caribbean." In Rice (1962), 34–53.

Stewart, W. A. (1963). "Functional Distribution of Creole French in Haiti." *Georgetown University Monograph Series on Languages and Linguistics* 15:149–162.

Stewart, W. A. (1968). "A Sociolinguistic Typology for Describing National Multilingualism." In Fishman (1968b), 531–545.

Stokhof, W. A. L. (1973). *The Extinct East-Slovincian Kluki-Dialect.* The Hague: Mouton.

Stroud, C. (1978). "The Concept of Semilingualism." *Lund University Working Papers* 16:153–172.

Sussman, H. M., P. Franklin, and T. Simon (1982). "Bilingual Speech: Bilateral Control?" *Brain and Language* 15:125–142.

Taylor, D. (1956). "Language Contacts in the West Indies." *Word* 12:391–414.

Taylor, D. (1957). "Review of *Spanish Contact Vernaculars in the Philippine Islands* by Keith Whinnom." *Word* 13:489–499.

Taylor, D. (1960). "Language Shift or Changing Relationship." *International Journal of American Linguistics* 26:155–161.

Taylor, D. (1961). "New Languages for Old in the West Indies." *Comparative Studies in Society and History* 3:277–288. Reprinted in Fishman (1968b), 607–619.

Taylor, I. (1971). "How Are Words from Two Languages Organized in Bilinguals' Memory?" *Canadian Journal of Psychology* 25:228–240.

Taylor, I. (1976). "Similarity between French and English Words: A Factor to Be Considered in Bilingual Language Behavior?" *Journal of Psycholinguistic Research* 5:85–94.

Teschner, R. V., G. D. Bills, and J. R. Craddock, eds. (1975). *Spanish and English of United States Hispanos: A Critical, Annotated Linguistic Bibliography.* Arlington, Va.: Center for Applied Linguistics.

Thomason, S. G. (1983). "Chinook Jargon in Areal and Historical Context." *Language* 59:820–870.

Thomason, S. G., and T. Kaufman (1977). *Language Contact, Creolization, and Genetic Linguistics.* Ms., University of Pittsburgh.

Thompson, R. W. (1961). "A Note on Some Possible Affinities between the Creole Dialects of the Old World and Those of the New." In Le Page (1961), 107–113.

Tollefson, J. W. (1981). *The Language Situation and Language Policy in Slovenia.* Washington, D.C.: University Press of America.

Tonkin, E. (1971). "Some Coastal Pidgins of West Africa." In Ardener (1971), 129–155.

Toporosic, J. (1981). "Slowenisch-deutsche Sprachkontakte." In Ureland (1981), 69–80.

Trim, R. (1981). "Central Old Belgium." In Ureland (1981), 237–250.

Troike, R. C., and N. Modiano, eds. (1975). *Proceedings of the First Inter-American Conference on Bilingual Education.* Washington, D.C.: Center for Applied Linguistics.

Trubetzkoy, N. S. (1939). *Grundzüge der Phonologie.* 3rd ed., 1961. Göttingen: Vandenhoeck & Ruprecht.

Tulving, E., and V. A. Colotla (1970). "Free Recall of Bilingual Lists." *Cognitive Psychology* 1:86–98.

Ureland, P. S. (1978). *Sprachkontakte im Nordseegebiet.* (Linguistische Arbeiten 66.) Tübingen: Max Niemeyer Verlag.

Ureland, P. S., ed. (1981). *Kulturelle und sprachliche Minderheiten in Europa: Akten des 4. Symposiums über Sprachkontakt in Europa, Mannheim 1980.* Tübingen: Max Niemeyer Verlag.

Ureland, P. S., and I. Clarkson, eds. (1984). *Scandinavian Language Contacts.* Cambridge: Cambridge University Press.

Vaid, J., and F. Genesee (1980). "Neuropsychological Approaches to Bilingualism: A Critical Review." *Canadian Journal of Psychology* 34:4–32.

Valdman, A., ed. (1972). *Papers in Linguistics and Phonetics to the Memory of Pierre Delattre.* The Hague: Mouton.

Valdman, A., ed. (1977). *Pidgin and Creole Linguistics.* Bloomington, Ind.: Indiana University Press.

Veenker, W. (1967). *Die Frage des finnougrischen Substrats in der russischen Sprache.* (Indiana University Publications, Uralic and Altaic Series 82.) Bloomington, Ind.: Indiana University Press.

Veltman, C. (1983). *Language Shift in the United States.* Hawthorne, N.Y.: Mouton de Gruyter.

Viitso, T.-R. (1974). "On the Phonological Role of Stress, Quantity, and StOd in Livonian." *Soviet Finno-Ugric Studies* 10.3:159–170.

Wanner, E. (1970). "Substratum as a Special Case of Grammar Simplification." *Papers in Linguistics* 2:415–448.

Weinreich, U. (1953). *Languages in Contact.* New York: Linguistic Circle of New York.

Weinreich, U. (1957a). "Research Frontiers in Bilingualism Studies." In *Proceedings of the 8th International Congress of Linguists,* 786–810. Oslo.

Weinreich, U. (1957b). "On the Description of Phonic Interference." *Word* 13:1–11.

Weinreich, U. (1958). "On the Compatibility of Genetic Relationship and Convergent Development." *Word* 14:374–379.

Weinstock, J., ed. (1978). *The Nordic Languages and Modern Linguistics* 3. Austin, Tex.: University of Texas Press.

Werner, R., ed. (1980). *Sprachkontakte*. Tübingen: Gunter Narr Verlag.

Whinnom, K. (1956). *Spanish Contact Vernaculars in the Philippine Islands.* Hong Kong: Hong Kong University Press.

Whinnom, K. (1965). "The Origin of the European-based Creoles and Pidgins." *Orbis* 14:509–527.

Whiteley, W. H. (1971a). "A Note on Multilingualism." In Ardener (1971), 121–127.

Whiteley, W. H., ed. (1971b). *Language Use and Social Change*. London: Oxford University Press.

Williams, L. (1974). "Speech Perception and Production as a Function of Exposure to a Second Language." Doctoral dissertation, Harvard University.

Williams, L. (1977). "The Perception of Stop Consonant Voicing by Spanish-English Bilinguals." *Perception and Psychophysics* 21:289–297.

Wolfard, H. C., and S. M. Shrofel (1977). "Aspects of Cree Interference in Island Lake Ojibwa." In Cowan (1977), 156–167.

Wolfson, N., and J. Manes, eds. (1985). *Language of Inequality.* (Contributions to the Sociology of Language 36.) New York: Mouton.

Yadrick, A. M., and D. H. Kausler (1974). "Verbal Discrimination Learning for Bilingual Lists." *Journal of Experimental Psychology* 102:899–900.

Young, R. K., and M. I. Navar (1968). "Retroactive Inhibition with Bilinguals." *Journal of Experimental Psychology* 77:109–115.

Young, R. K., and J. Saegert (1966). "Transfer with Bilinguals." *Psychonomic Science* 6:161–162.

Zeps, V. J. (1962). *Latvian and Finnic Linguistic Convergences.* (Indiana University Publications, Uralic and Altaic Series 9.) Bloomington, Ind.: Indiana University Press.

Index

Adstratum, 61
Albert, M. L., 29, 35, 36, 40, 41, 43
Arthur, B., 50
Arzapalo, R., 52

Balkanism, 61
Balkan Sprachbund, 61–65
Baltic Sea Sprachbund, 65–75
Bannert, R., 75
Beltramo, A. F., 23, 25, 26, 27
Bickerton, D., 83
Bilingual, 1, 23, 28–42
 compound bilingual, 29–42
 coordinate bilingual, 29–42
Bilingualism, 28–42
Blend, 21
Bloomfield, L., 78
Bourhis, R. Y., 50
Bradford, G., 50
Broch, I., 79
Bruce, G., 75
Buchwald, S. E., 11, 13

Calque, 20
Caramazza, A., 9, 11
Cassidy, F. B., 81
Cisneros, R., 58

Civ'jan, T. V., 64–65
Clyne, M., 14, 24, 25, 32, 58, 88
Code switching, 2, 22–25
Cohen, A. D., 23, 27
Communicative competence, 45
Contrastive analysis, 18–19
Creole, 76–88
 creolization, abrupt, 84
Crosby, C., 33, 36

Danforth, D. G., 71
DeCamp, D., 79
Decreolization, 87–88
Décsy, G., 69
Denison, N., 53–54
de Porcel, A., 25, 26
de Sivers, F., 69
Diehl, R. L., 11, 13
Diglossia, 45–46

Eek, A., 70
Elias-Olivarez, L., 58
Elman, J. L., 11, 13
Endzelin, J., 67, 68
Error analysis, 18–19
Ervin, S. M., 29

Espinosa, A. M., 23
Evers, K. W., 35, 36

Farrar, D., 50
Fasold, R. W., 58
Ferguson, C. A., 45
Filipović, R., 18
Foreign accent, 2, 4–5

Gal, S., 58
Gårding, E., 75
Genesee, F., 41
Giles, H., 50
Gloning, I., 41
Gloning, K., 41
Grosjean, F., 43
Gumperz, J. J., 23, 24, 75
Guttierrez, J. R., 58

Hall, R., 78, 82, 91
Hancock, I. F., 79, 82
Haugen, E., 13–14, 20, 23, 27, 28
Havelka, J., 33, 36
Hentrich, K., 72
Heras, I., 38, 39
Hernandez-Chavez, E., 23, 27
Hernandez, E., 23, 24
Hornby, P. A., 43
Hybrid, 21
Hymes, D., 45, 91
Hypercorrection, 8
Hypercreolization, 86

Ianco-Worrall, A. D., 37, 38
Inglehart, R. F., 54
Interference, 1–27
 grammatical interference, 13–15
 lexical interference, 19–27
 morphological interference, 13–15
 phonic interference, 2–13

phonotactic interference, 6–8
syntactic interference, 15–18
Ivić, P., 63

Jahr, E. H., 79
Jakobson, R., 59, 65, 66, 69, 75
Jargonization, 84–85

Kaufman, T., 84–85
Kolers, P. A., 33, 34, 35

Lambert, W. E., 33, 36, 42, 48–50
Lance. D. M.. 23. 24
Langendoen, D. T., 16
Language conflict, 54–58
Language loyalty, 46
Lehiste, Ilse, 16, 63, 65, 67, 70, 71, 72, 73, 75
Lekomceva, M. I., 68
Leone, E. A., 58
Leopold, W. F., 37
Linguistic affinity, 59
Lippus, U., 70, 71
Loanshift, 20
Loan translation, 20
Lorentz, F., 65–66

Mackey, W. F., 18
Matched guise technique, 48–52
Miracle, A. W., Jr., 43
Monogenetic theory, 79–82
Morpheme transfer, 19–20
Moverley, A. W., 82

Navarro-Tomas, T., 80
Nelde, P. H., 55
Nelson, K., 38, 39
Niemi, J., 74
Niemi, S., 74
Nikolaeva, T. M., 67

Index

Obler, L. K., 29, 35, 36, 40, 41, 43
Osgood, C. E., 28
Overdifferentiation, 5–6

Paradis, M., 43
Pidgin, 76–89
Pidginization, 88–90
Pitres's rule, 40
Polivanov, E. D., 70, 71
Polygenetic theory, 80, 82–83
Polyglot aphasia, 40–41
Postcreole community, 87–88
Posti, L., 69

Reinterpretation of distinctions, 6
Relexification, 80
Remmel, M., 70, 71
Rhodes, R., 77
Ribot's rule, 40
Rickford, J. R., 88
Riegel, Klaus F., 30
Ross, A.S.C., 82
Rūķe-Draviņa, V., 30, 32, 68

Sachs, J. S., 38, 39
Sandfeld, K., 75
Saville-Troike, M., 42
Schach, P., 58
Schaller, H. W., 61, 64, 75
Schuchardt, H., 81
Schumann, J. H., 46, 47, 48, 88–90, 91
Silverstein, M., 78, 82
Sorensen, A. P. Jr., 75
Sound substitution, 2–3
Sprachbund, 59, 60, 61
Stewart, W. A., 80, 81
Stimulus diffusion, 83
Stokhof, W. A. L., 65

Substratum, 60
Superstratum, 60

Taylor, I., 80
Thomason, S. G., 78, 82, 84–85
Thompson, R. W., 80
Thomsen, Vilhelm, 69
Transfer of rules, 3–4
Trubetzkoy, N. S., 59, 65, 70, 71
Tucker, G. R., 42

Underdifferentiation, 4–5, 14

Vaid, J., 41
Valdman, A., 76, 91
Veenker, W., 68
Veltman, C., 58
Viitso, T. -R., 69

Weinreich, U., 22, 27, 28
Whinnom, K., 80, 81
Whiteley, W. H., 27
Williams, Lee, 10, 11
Wilson, R., 75
Woodward, M., 54

Zeps, V. J., 67, 68, 69, 75
Zivian, Irina W. M., 30

www.ingramcontent.com/pod-product-compliance
Lightning Source LLC
Chambersburg PA
CBHW020750230426
43665CB00009B/556